TIGER IN THE SNOW

TIGER IN THE SNOW

The Life and Adventures of A. F. Mummery

by

WALTER UNSWORTH

LONDON
VICTOR GOLLANCZ LTD
1967

B67 06464

Printed in Great Britain by
The Camelot Press Ltd., London and Southampton

CONTENTS

Author's Preface 9

1. The Bear of Eisten 11
2. Race for the Zmutt 21
3. Matterhorn Again 35
4. Grépon 48
5. Interlude 59
6. Widening Horizons 68
7. Two Days on an Ice-slope 76
8. An Easy Day for a Lady 88
9. Guideless on Brenva 97
10. Death of a Tiger 108

Appendix: Mummery: Principal Dates and Climbs 121

Bibliography 126

LIST OF ILLUSTRATIONS

PLATES

	facing page
Mrs. Mummery	32
A. F. Mummery	32
A. F. Mummery with his daughter	32
The Matterhorn	33
The Grand Charmoz and Grépon ridges	64
The Charpoua face of the Aiguille Verte	65
Victorian climbers below the Requin	72
The Grépon Traverse	73
The Brenva face of Mont Blanc	88
Mummery leading the Mummery Crack	88
Nanga Parbat	89

MAPS AND DIAGRAMS

The Zmutt Arête	30
The Matterhorn	38
The Range of Mont Blanc	50
Dych Tau	74
Nanga Parbat	112

AUTHOR'S PREFACE

IN THIS BOOK I have tried to tell the story of A. F. Mummery, one of the greatest mountaineers who ever lived, and who, by his attitude to the sport, set alpine climbing on its modern course.

A considerable amount of detective work was necessary to establish the course of Mummery's career, for he was not a man much attracted to fame—he certainly did not climb for posterity—and even now many details of his Alpine adventures remain unknown. Every probable, and even improbable, link has been thoroughly explored by historians and it is unlikely that much more will be discovered.

The material I have freely drawn upon is listed in the bibliography. In addition, however, I would like especially to acknowledge my indebtedness to Mr. T. S. Blakeney of the Alpine Club for his considerable expert help over details. My thanks are also due to Messrs. A. K. Rawlinson (Hon. Sec. of the Alpine Club), Ian Clough, N. S. E. Pugsley (Exeter City Librarian) and John Kemsley, Hon. Librarian of the A.B.M.SAC, for the loan of Alexander Burgener's *Führerbuch*. Finally, my thanks are also due to the photographers whose names appear on the plates.

It is the duty of a biographer not merely to record facts but to draw conclusions from them. Any such conclusions in this book are entirely the author's responsibility.

CHAPTER ONE

THE BEAR OF EISTEN

ONE FINE SUMMER'S day in 1868 a group of excited Swiss schoolboys set out on the adventure of their young lives. They were spending a holiday in the remote but lovely Saastal which branches off the main Zermatt valley at Stalden, and the priest of the district—a funny old fellow called Imseng—had promised to take them on a mountain climb.

At first they had laughed amongst themselves at the idea of anyone so old and seemingly unworldly as the Abbé Imseng climbing a mountain, but their laughter stopped when they discovered that the learned old gentleman had been the first person to cross the high Mischabel range between Saas and Zermatt, and had also taken part in the first ascent of many of the peaks. Their respect for him grew—after all, a man who begins life as a humble shepherd, then learns French and Latin and becomes the parish priest, *and* the owner of three hotels, *and* a famous climber into the bargain, deserves a little respect.

On the morning of the expedition they quickly discovered another aspect of the Abbé's character—the old man had a steely discipline and powers of organisation beyond the ordinary. In no time at all he had the party lined up, ready to move off, with a word of reproof for the laggards, his eyes darting round to make sure everyone was properly equipped. When at last they were ready, he held up his hands for silence and introduced them to a newcomer, a young man in peasant clothes, scarcely much older than themselves.

"Today we climb the Mittaghorn," the priest announced, pointing towards a rocky spire dominating the village, "and this young man will be our guide. His name is Alexander Burgener, from Eisten, just down the valley. Nobody knows these mountains better than Alexander: follow him closely and do whatever he tells you."

The students looked at their new companion. Though scarcely twenty, Alexander Burgener appeared much older than his years. For one thing, Nature had not dealt with him kindly when she handed out her favours—he was enormously broad, but squat, with thick arms and legs and large capable hands telling of great power. His head, too, was built on the same lines, broad and with features which were downright ugly, including a bulbous nose. As if to hide as much as possible he had allowed his beard to grow up his cheeks and over his neck. Yet his eyes were bright and radiated good humour, giving him the overall appearance of an amiable teddy-bear.

The boys took to him at once. There was no question of his ability as a leader: one look at that massive frame, one glint from those confident eyes was enough to put courage into the faintest hearted. Why! They would have followed him up the dreaded Matterhorn had he given the word!

But the little Mittaghorn was their objective for the day and quite sufficient for a first expedition.

They followed their guide out of the chalets of Saasgrund, over the wooden bridge across the turbulent stream of the Saaser Visp, then up the steep winding track leading past the tiny shrines of the famous Kapellen Weg, until at last they were high above the main valley and entering the lush upland meadows of Fee.

From here the boys caught their first glimpse of the ice-draped peaks of the Mischabel, and if these giants among mountains made their own objective diminish in stature, they also impressed the boys with their beauty.

The way led on past the cowsheds of Fee, across a fiercely flowing torrent, then by numerous zigzags on the lower slopes of the Mittaghorn, until they came to a flat shoulder of the mountain which the Abbé called the Plattjen. Here they rested whilst Imseng tied up his greasy old cassock above his knees, revealing a disreputable pair of breeches, patched and faded. Quite obviously progress was going to become harder from the Plattjen onwards, and the old priest was making ready for it.

So it proved. From the Plattjen they stumbled over immense blocks of scree, round a corner of the mountain, then struck directly up towards a fearful looking precipice. There was a general murmur of excitement in the party, as, looking down, they could see the main valley stretched like a child's model thousands of feet below.

The way upwards seemed impossible, but Burgener led them cunningly through breaks in the cliffs, and progress proved not nearly as difficult as they had expected. True, it was steep and a slip would have been unpleasant, but there were plenty of good wide ledges on which to pause when they grew short of breath, and numerous sharp flakes of rock by the aid of which they could pull themselves up. The Abbé Imseng, they noted, easily kept pace with the party despite his sixty-two years, even prodding the slower members into greater efforts. As for Alexander, he just seemed to stroll up, leisurely and unconcerned.

Then, almost before they realised it, they were at the summit! A little gully gave out on to two sharp pinnacles of rock and the other side dropped away sheer to the meadows of Fee; a long, long way below. The Mittaghorn was theirs!

After their initial excitement had died, they settled down in various nooks and crannies to eat their bread and cheese, whilst the Abbé Imseng explained the panorama which lay before them like a map.

Far away in the north they could see the long line of the Bernese Oberland, with the Bietschorn looking like some distant white cloud. These mountains were separated from them by a long dark shadow which was all they could see of the deep trough of the Rhône valley. From this shadow the Vispertal stretched towards them, one arm becoming the Saastal, and the other, hidden from them by the high Mischabel mountains, was the long Mattertal, leading to Zermatt.

But it was the splendour of the mountains which attracted the boys the most. The old priest pointed out the beautiful snow cone of the Ulrichshorn, of which he had made the first ascent, the sharp, aptly named Nadelhorn, the Täschhorn, and the mighty Dom, highest mountain in all Switzerland.

These comprised the great Mischabel range, and they lapped in an arc round the little green oasis of Fee. Cattle, looking mere dots on the green carpet, fed contentedly on the rich pastures and there were a few hay stores of the typical Valaisan kind, but no hint was there that one day this little hanging valley would become a thriving holiday resort, rivalling Zermatt itself.

Below Fee ran the main Saastal, and beyond that again another range of fine peaks, not so high as the Mischabel, but very beautiful, especially the white cone of the Weissmies and the long jagged ridge of the Portjengrat.

The boys could have stayed for hours gazing at the superb panorama and listening to old Imseng tell tales of his adventures, but they still had to make their way down the mountain, and their guide was anxious to try a new route which he assured them was quick and safe.

The idea of descending where nobody had ever been before appealed to the students' spirit of adventure and they lent their eager support to Burgener, though Imseng was doubtful of the wisdom of venturing on unknown ground with such raw recruits. However, such were Alexander's powers of persuasion and his utter self-confidence that Imseng finally agreed, much to everyone's delight. Without more ado, Alexander jumped off down a snow-filled gully.

At first it was as Burgener had promised. The way was simple and they made rapid progress, but bit by bit the gully narrowed and steepened. The snow was soft and held their plunging footsteps, but gradually everyone sensed the serious nature of the work they had undertaken. Looking down, no one could have any illusions about what would happen should a slip occur!

They were not afraid; just excited and thrilled that the day was proving more adventurous than they had dared to hope. Their leader, for his part, grinned encouragement at them from time to time, hardly pausing in his downward course. He made even the steepest slopes look ridiculously easy.

Eventually the snow gave way to scree and they found themselves once again on the Fee meadows. Alexander had been right—it was a quick way down, and an exciting one. The boys cheered him for his brilliant effort.

Then the cheers froze on their lips. From behind the party, with the last stragglers, came old Imseng. His face was contorted with rage, his limbs shaking with emotion. The boys fell back, struck dumb by the priest's appearance. He marched straight up to the guide.

"Alexander Burgener," he cried, voice quivering with wrath, "you are an imbecile! A fool! What sort of mountaineer is it that leads his party down an avalanche couloir? Only by the grace of the good Lord above were we not all swept to oblivion! Call yourself guide? I call you fool! You will never make a good guide, Alexander Burgener. Never!"

Early in the August of 1870 a young man named Clinton Thomas Dent strode with purpose up the winding, dust-covered track leading from Stalden to Eisten in the Saastal.

Scarcely twenty years old, Clinton Dent was a very fortunate young man, born of wealthy parents and educated at Eton and

Cambridge. Moreover, he was a good-looking fellow with a pleasant freckled face, a small, neatly trimmed beard and bright wide eyes which reflected good humour.

Though he was wealthy enough to afford the finest clothes from the most fashionable London tailors, he was dressed on this occasion in the rough, travel-stained tweeds of the mountaineer, and on his feet were a pair of stout boots which he had designed himself and which hurt considerably as he walked. In one of his large sinewy hands he carried an ice-axe and on his back a knapsack stuffed with his requirements for the next few days.

Dent was on his way to meet a young guide he knew of called Burgener: a man reputed to be both daring and resourceful, quickly making a name for himself. Burgener sounded just the sort of guide Dent wanted—he was tired of following mediocre men up mediocre peaks.

During the fifties and sixties nearly all the really big mountains of the Alps had been climbed by the pioneers, and when Edward Whymper conquered the Matterhorn in 1865, only the Meije, in the remote Dauphiné, was left to defy man. Prophets were not wanting who declared that the Alps were played out— there was nothing left worth climbing—and consequently Alpine climbing would come to a speedy end.

But events proved otherwise. Even if there seemed to be no new climbs, there were plenty of new climbers. By 1870 the membership of the Alpine Club was almost double what it had been ten years previously.

The reason for this apparently uncalled for revival was the changing attitudes of the climbers to their chosen sport. The old-timers had been interested solely in conquering new peaks by the easiest possible route and the bigger the peak, the better they liked it. True, many of the biggest had provided tough struggles—the Matterhorn being a prime example—but the climbers did not go out of their way deliberately to seek difficulties. Gradually, however, the mood changed; for one thing, the big peaks were all climbed, and for another, climbers began to realise that there was more than one way of climbing a mountain, that the easiest way was not always the most enjoyable.

Consequently they began to direct their energies towards other ends—finding new ways on "old" peaks and climbing the many smaller but often formidable rock peaks which the

pioneers had disdained to climb. It seems incredible to us
nowadays that such splendid peaks as the Drus were totally
ignored because they were regarded as mere pinnacles on one
of the ridges of the Aiguille Verte!

Of course, this changing attitude towards climbing needed
much greater skill than the early pioneers ever possessed and
especially rock-climbing skill. It was often sufficient simply to
have a steady head and some scrambling agility to climb
mountains like the Rimpfischorn or even the Matterhorn when
a competent guide showed the way, but the newer climbs
demanded much more: the Portjengrat, the Drus, the Charmoz
—these, and the many similar climbs which were to be made
before the turn of the century, demanded genuine rock-
climbing skill, much more akin to that of the present day.

There was, however, one basic attitude to climbing which
hardly changed at all and that was the idea that every amateur
should be led by a professional guide. Though a few daring
spirits did climb without guides they were regarded as somewhat dangerous cranks—every responsible climber agreed that
no amateur could ever equal a guide in skill and knowledge of
mountaincraft.

Fortunately, the guides too were advancing with the times.
New men, born in districts where steep rock-climbing came as
second nature, began to make their mark as guides of repute.

Foremost were men of the Saastal, of whom Alexander
Burgener was undisputed leader. Born at Eisten, a tiny hamlet
clinging to the steep slopes below the Wannenhorn, in 1846,
Burgener had from earliest boyhood delighted to scramble and
explore the steep rocks and hidden cwms of his native valley.
There is no doubt at all that this childhood delight in the wild
places of Nature stayed with him throughout life and motivated
many of his daring adventures. Alexander was never in the
game just for the money.

By the time he reached his teens he had already acquired
local fame as a chamois hunter; a skill he was to retain all his life.

Anyone who has watched chamois in the Alps will know that
these beautiful animals are amazingly agile. Fast on their feet,
well camouflaged by nature, they inhabit the most inaccessibly
craggy places, leaping from ledge to ledge with apparent
unconcern. Hunting them is now severely restricted by law, but
in Burgener's day hunting chamois was a means of livelihood
for many Alpine peasants. To be successful a man had to match

the chamois in cunning, to be quick-witted, a good climber and a first-rate shot.

Strength counted, too. When a chamois was shot it had to be carried back to the village, often miles away across very rough country, and the usual method was to sling the animal around one's neck, feet foremost. Burgener, however, was stronger than average by a long way and even when he was sixty years old he managed to carry two chamois, one under each arm, for four hours across the mountains.

This early training undoubtedly gave Burgener a good start in life as a guide. From his knowledge of mountains and his great strength, stemmed his indomitable self-confidence which put such heart into his employers. Nothing daunted Alexander on a climb, simply because he could not conceive of a situation he could not handle.

But there is a world of difference between being just a good climber and being a good guide—a guide must estimate not only his own ability but that of his employer too, and in the early days Alexander was lacking in the experience necessary for this. Hence his fiasco with the schoolboys which brought down the wrath of old Imseng; and Clinton Dent, who was Burgener's first important employer, recalled in later years how he still shuddered at the thought of some of the narrow scrapes Alexander led him into.

Nevertheless, Dent and Burgener formed an ideal partnership. In their first year together they climbed the lovely Lenzspitze, one of the Mischabel peaks overlooked by the pioneers for some unaccountable reason. Then, in the following season, they climbed the Matterhorn together, still looked upon as a tough climb, and they made the first traverse of the Portjengrat, a magnificent rocky ridge on the Italian border of the Saastal.

In its way, the Portjengrat was symbolic of the new ideas in climbing. A small peak, entirely rocky, not as difficult as some of the Chamonix aiguilles which were to follow, it nevertheless offered rock-climbing of the most pleasurable kind. Ever since the day Burgener and Dent first climbed it, the Portjengrat has been one of the most popular climbs around Saas. It was miles away from the pioneers' ideas of climbing, but, as Dent pointed out: "The older members of the Club . . . have left us but these rock aiguilles. They have picked out the plums and left us the stones."

Meanwhile, as Dent and Burgener were cementing thei
partnership on the Matterhorn, a frail, short-sighted youth o
sixteen was gazing at that great mountain for the first time
Within him it stirred strange passions. He felt an overwhelming
desire to conquer it: to wrestle with its forbidding crags, t
traverse its majestic glaciers. He had never heard of Dent o
Burgener, nor they of him. He knew nothing of mountaineering
only that he wanted to climb. His name was Albert Frederich
Mummery.

In 1872 Burgener and Dent emphasised another aspect of the
new sort of climbing by ascending the Zinal Rothorn from
Zermatt. The mountain had been climbed many times from
Zinal, on the other side, but for years the Zermatt guides had
declared it impossible from their side. It was Burgener's idea
that they should make the attempt, and when it turned out to
be so successful, one might have expected the Zermatters to be
pleased, since it opened up a new route for the guides. Unfortunately, they were not pleased at all: they regarded Burgener's
ascent as something of a slap in the face to their professional pride.

Already there was bad blood between the men of the two
valleys, entirely caused by the jealousy of the Zermatt guides.
The plain fact was that whilst there was good money to be got
by guiding tourists up the traditional "big" peaks such as the
Matterhorn and Monte Rosa, the men of Zermatt were not
anxious to try new expeditions. At the same time they resented
the Saas men invading their territory and snatching prizes such
as the Zinal Rothorn from under their very noses!

The Zermatters' jealousy even went to the extent of slander—
they spread the rumour that the men of Saas cheated their
employers, especially that arch-villain Burgener. Martin
Conway, one of the best-known English climbers of the time,
did his best to scotch this ugly story by deliberately writing in
Burgener's *Führerbuch*, "Alexander is a thoroughly honest man".

The real nub of the whole matter was that Zermatt guiding
was at a low ebb, whilst that of neighbouring villages like
Täsch, Randa, St. Niklaus and the Saas hamlets was in the
ascendancy. The men of Saas, in particular, were coming to the
fore, and besides Burgener, names like Ferdinand Imseng,
Benedict Venetz and Johann Petrus were already becoming
well known. Had they but known it, the invisible threads of
fate were drawing them all towards that thin pale boy called
Mummery.

Alexander Burgener, meanwhile, was becoming famous throughout the Alps. Besides Dent, his clients numbered the cream of climbers from all over Europe; but far from being overawed by such talent, Alexander revelled in it. He knew that he was a match for any of them when it came to climbing —and he frequently told them so. His employers in their turn loved the great, shaggy-haired guide, for not only was he a very good climber but a great character as well; the source of more than one good after-dinner story. His roar of laughter matched that of a mountain torrent, and the way he would explode into a volume of loud oaths when meeting some unexpected difficulty was a constant source of amusement. Then, too, they appreciated the way in which he allowed them to climb— without tugging at the rope as some guides did—and even, if he thought they were good enough, to lead the easier parts.

In 1873, the year following the Rothorn ascent, Dent and Burgener began their famous siege of the Aiguille du Dru which was to last, on and off, for five years.

The Aiguille du Dru is one of the most impressive peaks in the Chamonix area. Seen from the hotel at Montenvers, which rests on a broad grassy shelf of mountain high above the village, the Dru looks for all the world like some gigantic stone spear-head. The idea that anyone could possibly climb it seems too ridiculous for words.

But of course this popular view of the Dru shows the mountain at its most dramatic. If you walk up the Mer de Glace, which lies like some great river of ice between Montenvers and the Dru, and then look back, an altogether different impression emerges. The mountain still looks formidable, but not inaccessible. This view gives a truer appreciation of what it really is—the termination of a long ridge descending from the Verte. From here, too, you can see that there are really two peaks—the Petit and Grand—with very little difference in height between them.

Time after time Dent and Burgener tried to climb the higher of the two Drus, and though they usually advanced a bit on each occasion, the climbing was much more difficult than anything they had ever tackled before. Like Whymper, when he tackled the Matterhorn, Dent began to despair of ever reaching the summit, but also like Whymper, he refused to admit defeat.

In the end his patience was rewarded. On his *nineteenth* attempt, September 11th, 1878, Dent, led by Alexander Burgener and accompanied by his friend J. W. Hartley and the guide Kaspar Maurer, reached the summit of the Grand Dru.

The conquest of the Dru set a new standard of alpine rock-climbing and was the finest achievement of Dent and Burgener. Though they climbed together in the Caucasus in later years, the Dru was their finest hour. It set the final seal of approval on Alexander's reputation. "He is one of the best, if not the best, guide in Switzerland," wrote Martin Conway in his *Führerbuch*. "Certainly the best guide to be found anywhere," added Oscar Eckenstein, another famous climber.

It seemed as though Alexander's cup was full, but he was intelligent enough to realise that the Dru was merely a beginning, not an end. He needed a partner who was his equal in ability and daring; but, as everyone said, he was the best in the world. To this he would laughingly agree until one day, when he was coming down a track near Zermatt with a great Hungarian mountaineer called Julius Kugy, he spied a tall thin man riding on a donkey. The man's long legs reached the ground on either side of the beast, his toes trailing in the dust. His face was pinched and he wore thick spectacles, indicating poor eyesight. His back was hunched as if against some cold draught, though the weather was warm, and altogether he presented a pitiable spectacle.

Kugy was moved to compassion. "Who is that poor fellow?" he demanded.

Burgener grinned. "That's Mummery," he replied. Then to Kugy's great astonishment added, "He climbs even better than I do."

CHAPTER TWO

RACE FOR THE ZMUTT

ALBERT FREDERICK MUMMERY was born on September 10th, 1855, in Dover, Kent.

The family had moved to Dover from Deal only five years before, when his father had purchased a tannery at Stembrook. They lived in an old Jacobean mansion known as Maison Dieu House, next to the Town Hall, where they followed the respectable middle-class traditions of Victorian England. The tannery flourished and in the course of time Mummery senior became Mayor of his adopted town.

Young Albert Frederick, however, gave rise to some parental anxiety. Either at birth, or shortly afterwards, he developed a weakness of the spine which in those days automatically classed him as a "sickly child", and there can be little doubt that he looked the part. Rather skinny and with increasingly myopic vision, he had the very opposite to that sturdiness of build which parents look for in their sons. Whether these mild deformities induced his father not to send him away for the usual public school education there is no means of knowing, for very little is recorded about his boyhood.

Certain it is that he grew into a rather ungainly youth—a fact of which he was well aware, for he hated to be photographed. On the other hand his disabilities did nothing to impair his spirit of adventure, his outstanding intelligence or his great sense of humour, and he must have been popular with his contemporaries.

In 1871, when he was sixteen, the family paid a visit to Switzerland, which was to influence Mummery for the rest of his life. He gazed in awe at the soaring crags of the Via Mala, above Thusis, and his young blood tingled with the sense of mystery and adventure presented by the wide snowfields and icy peaks of the high Alps. The climax came when, late one evening, he caught his first glimpse of the Matterhorn.

"It was shining in all the calm majesty of a September moon," he later wrote, "and, in the stillness of an autumn night, it seemed the very embodiment of mystery and a fitting dwelling-place for the spirits with which old legends people its stone-swept slopes."

For Mummery the Matterhorn became *the* mountain, a
though in the course of his life he was to climb it seven tim
and to tackle other mountains which were technically mu
more difficult, it always remained one of his favourit
Impressed though his young mind had been by everythi
which had gone before, it was the Matterhorn which co
clusively turned Mummery's steps towards a climbing care

When he first saw the Matterhorn he scarcely dared ho
ever to tread its summit, and yet three years later he did ju
that. It is one of his few early climbs of which we have any clu
for despite his ardent enthusiasm Mummery was not a shootin
star in the climbing firmament of his day. For eight years l
learned his craft patiently, often with indifferent guides
occasionally with good ones like Alois Burgener, Alexander
brother—all the time accumulating knowledge of the mou
tains. It was not easy: his disabilities prevented him fro
carrying heavy loads, so that he often had to engage an extr
man to do the work for him and his poor eyesight made hi
stumble, on the simplest path, over stones which only he coul
not see. He was the most unlikely looking prospect his guid
had ever seen, and his early attempts must have filled them wit
apprehension, both for his safety and theirs.

But Mummery learnt well; he probed not only the mour
tains but the capabilities of his own body until he knew i
strengths and its weaknesses. All his life he was to play the on
against the other, and play to the limit.

By the summer of 1879 this anonymous period of apprentice
ship was over, and towards the middle of August we find hir
crossing the Tiefmatten Joch, a steep col between the Den
d'Hérens and the Tête de Valpelline, regarding with interes
the unclimbed western slopes of the Matterhorn.

The Matterhorn's splendid obelisk has four faces, corres
ponding to the cardinal points of the compass. Where thes
meet they form four ridges, of which two, the Hörnli and th
Italian, pointing north-east and south-west respectively, hac
been climbed in 1865 and repeated many times since. Climber
had even traversed the peak—that is, ascended by one ridg
and descended by the other, but in the fourteen years which
had elapsed since 1865 nobody had tried to climb the Matterhorn by a *new* route.

This was not really surprising. The four enormous faces of
the mountain were periodically swept by cannonades of falling

rocks and avalanches, and the two remaining ridges looked almost equally formidable.

It was the Zmutt ridge, between the north and west faces, which caught Mummery's attention. It rises between glaciers as a slender snow arête ending abruptly at three giant pinnacles known as the Zmutt Teeth, which are easily discernible from Zermatt itself. From the Teeth the ridge goes much more steeply to a pronounced neb or nose which bars direct progress, then finally tapers off towards the summit.

That the snow ridge had the makings of a natural route had been obvious to the best guides for many years, but the problem of the overhanging nose seemed insuperable. One or two of the more daring spirits had thought of trying to force a passage, but none had actually done so. Most of them agreed with the sentiments of the great guide Melchior Anderegg, who, when asked whether the Zmutt would "go" replied, "Yes, it goes—but I'm not going!"

As Mummery strode down from the Stockje rocks on the track to Zermatt he took in every detail of the ridge and the west face. The more he looked the more certain did he become that the Matterhorn could be climbed that way—what matters a few pinnacles or an overhang? Difficulties existed only to be overcome—therein lay the adventure—and in any case he liked to regard things as a whole and leave the details until later.

His immediate need, before he could put any of his plans into operation, was for a guide of the first rank: a man not afraid to try a new climb and one whose skill matched his daring. In this Mummery had a piece of good luck, for as he entered Zermatt he met Alois Burgener who told him that Alexander was free of engagements and would probably welcome an opportunity to attempt the Zmutt. Mummery was delighted: the guide who had been with Dent on the Dru sounded just the man for the Matterhorn, and when the two met, Mummery was very impressed by the bear of Eisten.

As Mummery outlined his plans for the Zmutt, Burgener looked at him curiously. The *Herr* had not the usual athletic appearance of a young mountaineer, and though he had a good record of climbs to his credit he was not a member of the Alpine Club—in those days a very desirable qualification for anyone wanting a first-rate guide. Nevertheless, there was an indefinable something about the young Englishman which appealed to Alexander; perhaps it was the calm, methodical way in which he outlined his intentions, as though there was not the slightest doubt about success. If determination counted for anything the Englishman would certainly succeed. Burgener accepted Mummery's engagement.

But not to climb the Zmutt arête. "To attempt such a climb with a man I do not know would be the height of stupidity," he growled bluntly, and suggested that they should try something less ambitious for a start. Mummery realised the wisdom of this: Burgener's suggestion enhanced the Englishman's opinion of his guide. There had to be a period in which to build mutual trust, a time of testing between climber and guide to see whether they could form an effective partnership.

On Burgener's suggestion they crossed to the Saastal, where in the course of a week they repeated the Portjengrat climb, made the first traverse of a rocky arête called the Sonnigrat, and a rather desperate new crossing of the Fletschhorn which nobody repeated for fifty-three years!

This brief but exciting campaign removed from Burgener's mind any doubts he had about Mummery as a climber. Without more ado they returned to Zermatt for the attempt on the Zmutt.

The exertions of the past few days had taken greater toll of their energies than they thought at the time, so that when they reached Zermatt they felt in need of a rest-day and spent the last day of August lazing in some meadows near the village. The scent of the cut grass, the carpet of pale mauve autumn crocus and the chirruping of the cicadas combined to lull them into a sense of cosy peace: the Zmutt ridge could wait.

But that evening, as they strolled leisurely into the village, their complacency received a rude shock. Another party had set off for the Stockje rocks and rumour said they were intent on climbing the Zmutt ridge! Who were they? Mummery enquired, and his heart sank when he heard the name of William Penhall and the guides Ferdinand Imseng and Louis Zurbriggen.

William Penhall, twenty-one years old, was the wonder-boy of climbing at that time, with a career almost as meteoric as that of Whymper fifteen years earlier. His expeditions were daring, some said foolhardy, but of such difficulty that he had been elected to the Alpine Club at the age of eighteen. At Cambridge he was an enthusiastic gymnast under the instruction of George Passingham, from whom he may have first got the climbing urge, and in addition he was a rifle shot of international standard.

His chosen career was medicine and had he lived long enough for his talents to mature there is little doubt that he would have become an outstanding surgeon, for the qualities he brought to sport were just those needed for a good doctor: modesty, a cool head in emergencies and an extremely even temper.

Penhall's presence on the Zmutt ridge was virtually a cast-iron guarantee that the climb would be done, as Mummery well knew, but the two guides who were with Penhall made surety doubly sure.

In the first place, as chief guide, there was Ferdinand Imseng, the volatile little man from Macugnaga who was regarded by some as a guide in the same class as Alexander Burgener himself. The two men were about the same age, but very different in appearance and background. Imseng was dapper, with a pencil moustache and Italian features, much more refined than the bluff Burgener, and indeed he came from a family of modest fortune and had the benefit of a formal education.

Imseng was still only a porter in 1872 when he persuaded Richard Pendlebury at a chance meeting that they should attempt to climb Monte Rosa by its stupendous east face, the greatest ice-wall in the Alps. Pendlebury was game enough to try and the result was a brilliant success; the first ascent of what later became known as the Marinelli Couloir, still regarded today as a first-class expedition for experts. Imseng followed this with a series of brilliant exploits which quickly shot him to the forefront of his profession.

Though the second guide, Zurbriggen, was not in the same outstanding class as Penhall or Imseng, he was, nevertheless, a Saas man with a very good record; a counterbalance of experience to restrain the excesses of his mercurial companions.

When Mummery heard that these were the men who had gone to try the Zmutt ridge he had every right to feel despondent. Had he been Whymper, he would no doubt have set off at once in pursuit, if necessary alone, full of wrath and anguish and invoking the aid of the gods, but Mummery was of an altogether different stamp from the fiery pioneer. Mummery was much more cool and philosophical, with an air of detachment and a sense of humour that enabled him to laugh at the ironies of Fate. Now he calmly accepted the fact that Penhall would climb the Zmutt, and laid plans for a new route on the Dent Blanche instead.

In point of fact, Mummery had been misinformed about Penhall's activities, for that young man had not set out for the Zmutt at all, but was still in Zermatt! His guides, however, had been around the village collecting provisions and talking to their contemporaries, at the same time trying to lay a smoke-screen about their intentions. In this they were not very success-ful, since Imseng told one story and Zurbriggen another and the porter they had hired to carry their gear told yet a third. It didn't take the rest of the guides and the climbers long to work out that something big was afoot and since all the stories tallied on one point—that the party was going towards the Stockje—the knowledgeable ones put two and two together and came up with the obvious answer—the Zmutt ridge. What Mummery heard was probably a garbled version of these stories together with the assumption that Penhall had already started.

On the Monday morning of September 1st, Penhall rose at 2.30 to find that the clouds were low in the valley with not a star in sight. Nevertheless, he collected his party and provisions and set off hopefully for the mountain. As they trudged in the dark through the hamlets of Winkelmatten and Zmutt they looked for an improvement in the weather, but none came, and by the time they reached Stafel it was if anything even more unpromising, so they sought out a hay-loft and went to sleep.

About 7.30 a.m. they awoke to find that though the weather was still unsettled the clouds had lifted from the Matterhorn, and this encouraged them to start once more.

Their first objective was the graceful snowy arête which is such a prominent feature of the route. This they reached with-out much trouble, but once on the ridge they were surprised to find that the seemingly easy snow crest consisted of hard ice which required strenuous step-cutting all the way to the Zmutt Teeth. This took them two hours, so that by the time they reached the real difficulties the day was already advancing.

The porter who had accompanied them thus far was now left with the provisions and blankets at the first of the teeth whilst Penhall and the guides went ahead to explore. They found the first and second of the pinnacles easy to cross, the third a bit more difficult, but then they were confronted by what appeared an impassable gap. Beyond the gap the ridge was patently unclimbable and the only route seemed to go to the left, by a flanking movement, up a nasty looking couloir. Obviously these problems were going to take time to solve—time they did not have. By a unanimous decision they decided to go back along the snow arête, find a bivouac spot for the night and try again on the morrow.

It was a bitterly cold night. Cramped on a tiny ledge at the lower end of the snow arête they found sleep impossible and sought to fight off the cold by making incessant brews of hot chocolate and mulled wine, sheltered from the wind by a blanket, until finally their stove ran out of fuel and they were reduced to waiting miserably for the dawn.

What little hope they had of continuing their climb vanished with daybreak. The wind increased and it began snowing. It became imperative that they retreat from the mountain altogether before frostbite and other effects of exposure set in. Taking a direct line down to the glacier without more ado, they continued in retreat towards Zermatt.

At the Stafelalp they met Mummery and his guides coming up from Zermatt to do their projected ascent of the Dent Blanche. Penhall was somewhat surprised that Mummery should be setting out when the weather signs were so obviously bad, and as they passed the time of day he mentioned this, saying that his guides agreed the only sensible course was to return to the village. Mummery replied that this was so, but now he had come so far he might as well go to the hut at the Stockje in the faint hope that the weather would improve.

So they parted on their separate ways, and as Penhall disappeared round a bend in the track towards Zermatt, Mummery's mind saw at once that here was a chance to snatch the Zmutt.

Mummery was always master of the half-chance and he took a half-chance now. With him he had Alexander Burgener and the nineteen-year-old Augustin Gentinetta, with enough provisions for ten hours. He determined to go to the Stockje, ride out the threatened storm, then make a quick dash for the Zmutt before Penhall could return from Zermatt. In order to do this he had to overcome two difficulties—first, to convince his guides that the weather would improve and, secondly, secure more provisions for a longer stay.

The first of these problems demanded all Mummery's skill.

By the time they reached the Stockje the weather was looking so poor that Burgener suggested they should return at once to Zermatt. Mummery, however, feigned surprise at such an idea and supporting his arguments with meteorological theories which he made up on the spot, sought to convince the guides that high winds and thick clouds meant that good weather was on the way.

So forcibly did he argue, and so confident his manner, that Burgener was half convinced, despite all his experience to the contrary, and he agreed to stay. Young Gentinetta, however, stuck stubbornly to his own view that the weather would become worse, and Mummery, realising that the young guide might make Burgener change his mind, adroitly ordered him to return to Zermatt for more provisions and another man to help them. . . . "We felt that the exercise might be good for his spirits," Mummery wrote, tongue in cheek, "and that in any case his company would be depressing."

As the day wore on the weather became ever more threatening and Burgener began to think that his employer was either a madman or divinely gifted with second sight. For his own part Mummery went to sleep, hoping as always for the best, but secretly fearing the worst. Late in the afternoon he was awakened by a violent thump between the shoulder-blades from Alexander. Half asleep, Mummery at first thought that the threatened storm had broken and Burgener was punching him in anger, but a moment later he could see that the guide was jumping for joy, his ugly face wreathed in smiles! What a remarkable weather prophet Herr Mummery was, cried Alexander: the storm had cleared away and the evening was fine!

Now thoroughly awake, Mummery could scarcely believe his good fortune, but it was indeed as Burgener said—the clouds had gone and there was the Matterhorn in first-rate condition.

Burgener thought the whole affair miraculous. All his years spent in the mountains, watching the weather day in and day out, had told him that a storm was coming. Not only that, but Gentinetta had said so too, and Imseng, and Zurbriggen, but Herr Mummery knew better. What a weather prophet! And though on many future occasions Mummery was wrong in his weather forecasts, nothing shook Burgener's opinion that his employer was the greatest forecaster in the world.

Now that the weather had improved they could go ahead with their plans. Gathering together their belongings they left the hut and crossed over to the Schönbeil rocks where they had agreed to await the return of Gentinetta, and at about 8 p.m. the young guide appeared, all apologetic for having doubted Mummery's weather wisdom, and bringing with him Johann Petrus as extra man.

The half-chance was paying off. Johann Petrus made a strong team even stronger—a quick-tempered neighbour of Alexander's at Eisten, but a brilliant rock-climber, exceptionally strong. Mummery had no doubt that on the morrow the Zmutt ridge would be conquered.

But meanwhile, in Zermatt, their rivals were having second thoughts. When Penhall first reached the village some spots of rain had begun to fall, making him glad that he had not followed Mummery's example of spending the night at the Stockje, but the storm failed to materialise and at about 6 p.m. Imseng came to him with a forecast of good weather, and urged that they should start for the Matterhorn at once.

The suggestion took even the dynamic Penhall aback. Why such urgency? They had been on the go for two whole days with no sleep worthy of the name, surely the Zmutt could wait? There was no knowing for certain that Mummery would try the climb (he had intended to climb the Dent Blanche, remember) and even if he did, Penhall was willing to concede him victory by the fortunes of war. "I should hardly have proposed it myself," he wrote, when later describing Imseng's proposition. And this reveals the real instigator of the race for the Zmutt—Ferdinand Imseng, guide of Macugnaga!

Whether Imseng was determined to beat the great Alexander Burgener to the top, or whether he was simply annoyed with himself at having so misjudged the weather, we shall never know, but it was Imseng rather than the placid Penhall who determined to race Mummery for the top.

When Penhall recovered from the first shock of the suggestion his competitive spirit came to the fore and he at once agreed. So it was that at 10 p.m. his party set out once again for the Zmutt, along the now familiar path. They rested for twenty minutes when they were clear of the pine woods, then pushed on remorselessly towards the glacier. They did not halt again until 3.30 a.m., when they stopped an hour for breakfast, having reached the foot of the Zmutt arête.

By means of this prodigious forced march Penhall's party was in fact ahead of Mummery who was still sleeping on the Schönbeil rocks, but Imseng did not know this. From his tactics later in the day it seems apparent that he assumed Mummery would bivouac on the ridge itself, just as he had done the previous night. Had he but known it, he had the climb within his grasp, only to throw it away.

Mummery and his party quit their bitterly cold bivouac as soon as there was enough light to see by. They made straight for the arête and must have missed Penhall by just a few minutes, though of course they were quite unaware of their rival's return. At 5.20 a.m. they came upon the site of Penhall's original bivouac, where they left some blankets in case they too were forced to spend a night on the ridge.

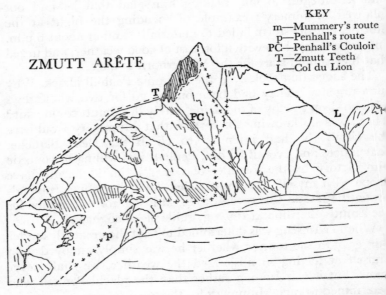

ZMUTT ARÊTE

KEY
m—Mummery's route
p—Penhall's route
PC—Penhall's Couloir
T—Zmutt Teeth
L—Col du Lion

After a half-hour's halt for breakfast they made short work of the snow arête, aided no doubt by the steps which their predecessors had so laboriously cut two days before, crossed the first two pinnacles of the Teeth and came to a halt at the gap which had stopped Penhall.

The way ahead looked extremely unpleasant. A deep gap separated them from the next part of the ridge and though they reckoned they could climb into this, the only way on from there was by some dangerously loose slopes on the left. Like Penhall, they thought the ridge itself unclimbable.

For three-quarters-of-an-hour they remained gathered on top of the third pinnacle, undecided whether or not to go on. Suddenly, the stillness of the morning air was broken by a distant yodel and looking down they spied Penhall on the west face. It acted like a shot of adrenalin, galvanising them into immediate action.

They descended into the gap and found to their relief that the escape route which seemed so formidable was not really too bad. Soon they were past it, only to discover an even nastier piece of climbing barring their way.

For once, Burgener faltered, declaring himself in favour of retreat, not because he couldn't climb it but because there was absolutely no way of holding a slip if one should occur and he did not wish to place Mummery's life in jeopardy. But Mummery would have none of this and in the end it was agreed that Johann Petrus should go ahead, solo; Burgener would then bring up Mummery on the rope, and young Gentinetta would fetch up the rear by himself. To a modern climber such an arrangement appears fantastic, but in those days rope technique was scarcely understood even by the best climbers.

Fortunately, the climbing soon became easier and they scrambled up to the great overhanging nose where they snatched a rest.

These dangerous excursions to the left of the ridge were found by later climbers to be unnecessary, but it is the fate of pioneers that they must take the line which looks most obvious. Not knowing what difficulties might lie ahead they have no time to waste trying ways which look hard.

Whilst Mummery and his guides were engaged on the ridge, Penhall, Imseng and Zurbriggen were finding difficulties of their own.

You will remember that they had breakfasted at 3.30 a.m. at the foot of the ridge and the way ahead, following their old tracks, lay open to them. Imseng, however, or perhaps Penhall, must have assumed that Mummery was in front of them, and they had not walked all the way back from Zermatt simply to follow Mummery. They intended to be first, not second.

Imseng therefore led the party off on a most curious route, the sole intention of which was to outflank Mummery and beat him to the top. His intention was to omit the lower snow arête and the *mauvais pas* beyond the Teeth by making a bee-line up the west face for the top part of the Zmutt ridge.

It was a daring plan, dangerous too, because the west face suffered from regular bombardments of falling stones, but the sort of plan for which Ferdinand Imseng was notorious.

Penhall seems not to have objected, however, so in the pale morning light they crept along the foot of the ridge until they came to an enormous couloir which descends to the glacier from the Zmutt Teeth. This couloir, now called Penhall's Couloir, is a natural chute for any stones falling on this side of the Matterhorn; a certain death-trap for anyone foolish enough to try climbing it. Even Imseng was not that mad, of course, but simply to *cross* the couloir involved considerable danger.

Yet cross it they must. The foot of the couloir was too wide for safety, so they climbed up the loose rocks of its left side until eventually they came to a place where it narrowed. They now had to risk everything. Could they cross the tantalising ribbon of snow in safety, or would they be swept off the face of the mountain by an avalanche of rocks? Twelve steps, that was all it needed, twelve steps—and luck.

Five minutes later all three were across, breathing relief. Now they were committed: there could be no turning back.

They found themselves on an area of steep slabs down which rocks skipped and hummed intermittently throughout the day. The climbing, however, was not difficult, and though Penhall dropped his ice-axe and watched it go bounding through space to the distant glacier, they made good progress without any further incident. It seemed as though the outflanking movement was paying rewards, for as they steadily advanced they could spy Mummery halted at the Zmutt Teeth. They gave him a joyous yodel.

Soon, however, it was their turn to halt. They gathered on a narrow ledge, just about level with the Zmutt Teeth, looking with dismay at the impassable slabs above them. On their left the rocks looked formidable, too, so they decided to go to the right, simply because they could not see what lay in that direction. . . . Three-quarters-of-an-hour later they were only a hundred feet farther and two hours after that they were back at the ledge, disillusioned.

Mrs. Mummery

A. F. Mummery

A. F. Mummery with his daughter

(Photographs: courtesy the Alpine Journal)

THE MATTERHORN   The Furggen ridge is on the left and the Zmutt on the right.   The ordinary

There was nothing for it but to strike to the left over the great bowl-like couloir which is such a feature of this face. The climbing was desperate and on one occasion they were lucky to escape with their lives as an avalanche of rocks narrowly missed them. They had only one hope—to reach the Galérie Carrel, a curious ledge which encircles the upper part of the west face, and where they would be relatively safe.

By this time, Mummery too had been forced out on to the west face by the difficulties of the ridge, but the Tiefmatten Slabs upon which he found himself were not nearly as difficult as those Penhall was struggling with. With Petrus still leaping ahead unroped, Burgener bringing up Mummery on the rope, and Gentinetta fetching up the rear, they climbed steadily towards the Galérie Carrel.

Carrel's Ledge, or at least that part which gave access to the Zmutt ridge, proved trickier than they had expected—but nothing could stop them now. Soon they were over the difficulties, the rocks became easier and easier and at 1.45 p.m. they reached the Italian summit of the Matterhorn. The Zmutt ridge was conquered.

But where was Penhall? As Mummery descended the ordinary route he caught sight of his rivals just emerging on to the crest of the Zmutt ridge after their desperate ascent of the west face. He yodelled across the void to let them know the day had been won.

Penhall reached the summit at 3 p.m., or about an hour and a quarter after Mummery. The race had been close and gallantly fought and the honours were even. True, Mummery won because of better tactics, but Penhall's performance was still a remarkable one—he had reached the summit of the Matterhorn by a new and difficult route direct from Zermatt in seventeen hours, and after being almost continuously on the move for three days and nights.

Of the two routes there is no doubt that Mummery's is the finest and safest, regarded by modern climbers as one of the classic Alpine climbs. On the other hand, Penhall's climb has lived up to its reputation for danger, and as far as is known there has only ever been one other ascent in all the years since Penhall and Imseng made their great effort.

The first ascent of the Zmutt ridge brought Mummery spectacularly to the forefront of Alpine climbing and established the great partnership with Burgener which was to

B

dominate the Alpine scene for the next two years. It should have been a source of pride to Mummery all his life, yet, sad to tell, this great climb was later used by unscrupulous persons to blacken his character; and when he made out his application form to join the Alpine Club he did not even mention it.

CHAPTER THREE

MATTERHORN AGAIN

A FEW DAYS AFTER the race for the Zmutt arête, Mummery and Penhall, with their respective guides, made a joint ascent of the Dürrenhorn, an easy peak in the Mischabel group. They had mistaken their mountain for the nearby Nadelhorn, and though the ascent was completely without incident it is significant as being the first one that Mummery made with a friend—all his previous climbs had been with guides alone.

It seems likely that about this time Penhall would have brought up the question of Alpine Club membership, coupled with the unusual fact that a man like Mummery, obviously well qualified to join, was not a member. And it *was* unusual, for almost every British climber in those days belonged to the Alpine Club, but it must be remembered that Mummery was always sensitive about his ungainly appearance and it could well be that this deterred him from seeking the company of more athletic looking mountaineers for fear they might mock him. He felt it necessary to prove his skill first in the company of guides.

There is no doubt that he longed to join the Club, and Penhall probably promised to help him. After the brilliant season culminating in his Zmutt success, his name was on everyone's lips and it was obvious that a new star had arisen in the climbing firmament.

Now it so happened that the Alpine Club, in common with most other clubs of the Victorian era, demanded of its members something more than mere ability. For membership, it helped to be wealthy, though money alone was not sufficient either: a man had to be respectable and socially acceptable to the other members. This last was really the nub of the whole matter, for if a man were a chimney-sweep or a shopkeeper, no amount of ability or wealth would get him elected. Lawyers, doctors, businessmen and bankers—these were the sort of men who formed the Alpine Club.

Mummery, of course, came within this category: he was part owner of a tannery in Dover, son of the Mayor, and well-to-do. There was no earthly reason why he should not be elected to the

Club with the minimum of formalities, especially as it happened that he was proposed by Clinton Dent, the Secretary, and seconded by Douglas Freshfield, the Vice-President. On March 18th, 1880, his application was passed by the Committee and it required only the final formality of the ballot-box.

On April 6th the ballot was held in the Club Rooms, those voting "Aye" using little white balls and those voting "No", black balls. When everyone had voted, the balls were counted and the result announced—*Mummery was rejected*!

Dent, Freshfield, Penhall and all the active progressive members were stunned. It seemed incredible, yet it was true— literally in black and white.

Quite obviously something had happened to turn the majority of members against Mummery, and his friends tried to find out what it was. Bit by bit the story was pieced together, though it was not for many years afterwards that the real facts of the "Mummery Plot" were made public.

It all stemmed from the jealousy of one man—William Edward Davidson, twenty-six years of age and a newly qualified barrister of the Inner Temple. Davidson's climbing career paralleled that of Mummery in several respects, except that whereas the latter went from success to success, Davidson never amounted to much when it came to new conquests. No doubt he resented the meteoric rise of Mummery, seeing in it a threat to his own influence within the Club, which was considerable. Nevertheless, he was one of the Committee that passed Mummery's application in March, even declaring himself a supporter of the new applicant.

Secretly, however, his jealousy had got the better of him and he worked for Mummery's downfall. As the recent Acting Secretary his opinions carried weight, so that it did not take him long to convince a considerable number of members that Mummery was unsuitable. It was subtly done: a hint here, a word there, perhaps the suggestion that Mummery had not been *quite* sporting in stealing the Zmutt after Penhall had done the work. Someone also started the rumour that Mummery was a tradesman, that his tannery was really only a shoe-shop in Dover; and though we might laugh at such ridiculous distinctions nowadays, it made a lot of difference in class-conscious Victorian society. Trade was regarded as inferior; there was no place for a tradesman in the select Alpine Club.

When Mummery heard he had been blackballed, all his old

fears came rushing back. He felt himself to be an outcast and he was torn between a longing to be a member of the Club and deep resentment of their rejection. His was a sensitive nature, easily hurt. Afraid of further rebuff he did not apply for membership again for eight years, and almost gave up climbing altogether.

But in the summer months following immediately upon his disappointment, his reaction was one of almost savage determination to succeed. Once more he turned to the one man he could trust, Alexander Burgener.

He went out to the Alps earlier than usual bent on a very full programme, and the end of June found him with Burgener, basking in the sunshine on the very rocks from which they had set off on their Zmutt climb the previous year.

They had just crossed the Col Tournanche from Breuil, and Mummery, looking back over the way they had come, allowed his gaze to wander along the full length of that stupendous mountain wall which stretches from the Matterhorn to the Tête de Valpelline. In particular his attention was caught by a steep and narrow couloir rising from the glacier to the Col du Lion.

Seen from where Mummery was sitting the Col du Lion is a prominent notch at the lower end of the Italian ridge of the Matterhorn, and in fact it is the proper starting-point for anyone who wishes to climb the mountain that way. It had been visited many times, of course, but always from Breuil on the other side, whence the ascent is easy. Nobody had climbed to the col from the Tiefmatten side and Mummery began to think it was high time somebody did.

When he broached the idea to Alexander, the guide almost choked on the Bouvier wine he was drinking. He pointed out that many good men had had the same idea, but they had all turned back after a closer look at the couloir. Even Tyndall and the great Whymper had declared it impossible, and, further, it was a veritable death-trap, due to that curse of the Matterhorn—falling stones.

Though Burgener was obviously not at all sympathetic to the plan, Mummery knew that Alexander almost always began by declaring everything impossible, unless he happened to think of it himself. He knew too that the guide could be won round by patience and cunning. So with a little flattery here and cajolery there, and liberal helpings from the wine bottle, he set to work

on Alexander, and before the sun started to dip in the west
Burgener was agreeing that the Col du Lion would make a
splendid climb.

When they returned to the village, however, they found
news awaiting them of a death in the Burgener family which
necessitated Alexander's absence. Mummery kicked his heels
impatiently until Burgener returned on July 5th, and since the
weather was still holding out, they decided to start that same
evening.

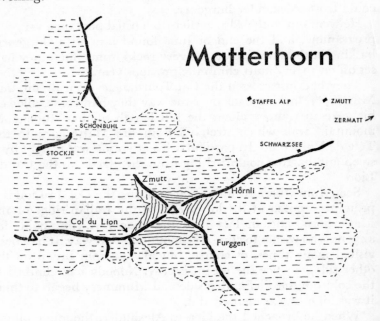

Matterhorn

STAFFEL ALP   ZMUTT

ZERMATT

SCHÖNBUHL

SCHWARZSEE

STOCKJE

Zmutt

Hörnli

Col du Lion

Furggen

Ten o'clock was the time arranged for departure, but when
that hour arrived Mummery overslept and was nearly an hour
late. Then they discovered that they had no rope, each
expecting the other to bring one, and a quick search of the hotel
failed to bring one to light. Undaunted, they began a tour of
the village, where everyone was sound asleep, knocking on
doors in the hope of borrowing or buying a rope from one of
the guides. All they got for their efforts was loud abuse; in the
first place the guides resented being dragged from their beds by
fools who had forgotten to get a rope, and in the second place
no Zermatt guide in his right mind would lend his arch enemy
Burgener a rope!

Feeling defeated even before they had begun the climb, Mummery and Burgener returned to the hotel in towering bad tempers. They gave expression to their wrath by grabbing the unfortunate night porter and blaming all their misfortunes on him—after all, he *had* forgotten to wake Mummery at the right hour! Terrified that they might tear the Monte Rosa Hotel apart with their bare hands, the porter suddenly remembered that he had been entrusted with the safe keeping of a rope for another guest. Mummery didn't care a fig who the rope belonged to—he grabbed it, and at last he and Burgener started for the Matterhorn. The time was 1 a.m.

As the first weak rays of dawn touched the tip of the Matterhorn they made their way over the ice of the Tiefmatten Glacier towards the formidable Couloir du Lion.

The nearer they came to their objective the more impregnable it seemed. Its foot was guarded by an immense bergschrund, cutting it off from the glacier like the moat of a castle. Some three hundred feet above this the couloir bulged with overhanging rocks upon which they could detect layers of green water-ice, totally impossible of assault.

They could readily appreciate why their predecessors had not attempted the couloir, it looked so hopeless, but both Mummery and Burgener found hopeless situations stimulating. Where there is a will there is usually a way, and as they peered up at the dark recesses of the icy chasm they could see a possible line avoiding the ugly bulges of ice. A convenient snow bridge helped them over the bergschrund.

At first Mummery took the lead to save Alexander's strength for the more difficult climbing. He followed the course they had plotted from below and found that their way, to the right of the couloir, was indeed a practical one for avoiding the ice bulges. But then they had to traverse back into the gully bed and this required delicate balance and iron nerves. Inch by inch, with Burgener now in command, they edged towards their goal. It was so steep that they could not pass one foot behind the other and were forced to change step on every foothold.

After what seemed an eternity they finally reached the bed of the couloir. It was dark and cold, hemmed in by precipitous rock-walls soaring to the mountains which formed either flank. They were conscious that these same walls also showered stones into the gully once the sun's rays loosened the binding night-frost, so they hurried upwards as fast as they dared.

Sometimes they were climbing on bare water-ice where the axe shuddered at every blow as though it were striking steel, and where steps were reduced to mere notches. At other times progress was made easy by packed ribbon-snow into which they could kick steps with their boots. But all the time the going was extremely steep, and they were racing against the clock.

Then they noticed the barrier. Up above, dark ice-coated overhangs jutted out from the bed of the couloir.

"Can we get up, Alexander?" Mummery asked anxiously.

"We must, Herr Mummery, otherwise we'll both be finished," the guide answered, gravely. Time did not allow for any retreat at this stage.

By this time Burgener's hands were cut and bleeding from contact with the ice. Mummery took over the lead.

The rocks of the couloir entirely blocked the centre of the passage, but left on each side narrow, ice-filled grooves of desperate steepness. That on the right looked the easier of the two, but unfortunately the sun was already warming the rocks on that side and small stones and icicles had started hissing down it. The only way was to the left, still mercifully in shadow.

Burgener took the lead again. The climbing was on steep, hard ice, every step demanding vigorous blows with the axe; progress was slow. But he kept at it until, when he was almost a hundred feet above Mummery, he suddenly stopped and let out a volley of the strongest Swiss oaths. Burgener's axe had broken!

The situation was one of great danger. They were trapped in the couloir, with difficult climbing ahead, no means of retreat, and only one sound axe between them.

There was no question as to who should have the remaining axe. As leader, Burgener needed it to cut steps, and so Mummery untied himself from the rope, fastened his axe on the loose end and sent it up to Alexander. Burgener then dropped the rope-end back to his employer, but to Mummery's dismay it caught on the rocks eighty feet above him. Desperately, Burgener tried to free the rope, but it would not budge. Every minute the sun was climbing higher into the sky—being trapped in the couloir was like sitting on a time bomb.

Mummery's superbly cool brain worked out their dangers and calculated the risks in an instant. There was not a moment to lose: he had to get the rope.

Without an ice-axe, without crampons—he was wearing

ordinary nailed boots—Mummery began climbing eighty feet of the most difficult ice in the Alps. One slip and he would have hurtled hundreds of feet to the glacier; one chance falling stone, no matter how small, and he would have been a dead man. But no stones fell and he didn't slip. He climbed coolly and calmly until at last he could grasp the end of the rope and tie himself on again.

It was an incredible performance, demonstrating not only Mummery's superb skill but also his nerves of tempered steel.

When at last he rejoined the thankful Burgener, he took charge of the shattered axe. It wasn't much good, but at least it was better than climbing with bare hands!

They now found themselves at the top of their gully, level with the upper reaches of the overhanging rocks, but trapped in a sort of blind alley. In order to continue they had to traverse to the right over vertical rocks thickly glazed with ice. It looked more difficult than anything they had yet attempted, and Burgener, cracking under the strain, suggested retreat. But as Mummery was quick to point out, if retreat was impossible earlier on, it was certainly impossible now.

When he had fortified his nerves with a swig from Mummery's brandy flask, Burgener advanced on to the traverse. The ice coating the rocks was little more than thick verglas, iron hard and totally insufficient for step-cutting. In such a place even changing step from hold to hold was out of the question, so he cut a narrow ledge, sufficient to hold just two or three boot-nails, along which they could shuffle.

There was no room to swing his axe, no possibility of solid blows. Pressed hard against the vertical ice-coated rock, Burgener had to hang on to nicks he had cut for his left hand whilst he chipped away the little ledge with his right. It demanded enormous effort, a great strain on his right hand, and when he had finished his right wrist was painfully swollen.

Burgener's objective was a crest of snow which ran upwards from the top of the couloir rocks. When eventually he reached it he found to his dismay that it was loose powder snow, likely to slide off at any moment. Under normal circumstances no experienced climber would touch such dangerous stuff, but for Burgener there could be no going back. The snow *had* to hold. With his ponderous hands he compacted it down as hard as he could, then, with a muttered prayer, launched his great bulk on to the crest.

The gods favoured Burgener at that moment. The snow held.

When Mummery joined him they climbed quickly up much easier slopes towards the top of the couloir. Gone now was their fear of stones falling, they were entering into the wide funnel shaped top of the couloir above all possible stone-fall danger. After hours in the dark recesses they welcomed the change to spacious slopes and sunlit skies.

Nothing could stop them now! Up and up until they reached the final rock-wall which tops the couloir. This proved tricky, even dangerous, but with success literally within grasp they stormed every difficulty. The col was won!

With gasps of relief they collapsed on the snows of the col, thankful their ordeal was over, but exuberant at victory. First they attended to their fingers which were mildly frostbitten from uninterrupted contact with the ice for so long, and they suffered agonies as the warm blood coursed back. Then, too, Burgener's wrist needed bandaging as it was still swollen from the step-cutting. But these discomforts were adequately compensated for by the sense of achievement—by the knowledge that they had defeated yet another of the Matterhorn's formidable defences.

They yodelled and drank wine, and Alexander excitedly recalled the various episodes of the adventure.

After an hour's rest they began their descent to Breuil. Their object was to make a complete crossing of the Col du Lion and so, instead of taking the ordinary way down, they kept strictly to the couloir on the Italian side of the col. What a difference to the couloir they had climbed that morning! Here the snow was smooth, easy angled, and they could glissade most of the way. In an hour-and-three-quarters they were at Breuil.

In those days, Breuil was not the international ski and holiday resort it is now, with expensive shops and grand hotels, but a simple place consisting almost solely of the inn. Travellers might or might not find the place open, and food available, but if they wanted to be sure they had to send word in advance. Mummery was well aware of this, and he had taken the precaution of sending a man over the Théodule Pass from Zermatt to ensure a meal would be waiting for Burgener and himself when they had crossed the col.

So it was with some anticipation that they arrived at the inn, tired and hungry after their adventurous day. A good meal would set them to rights in no time, and the man they sent over had been warned to make sure the landlord had everything ready.

Unfortunately, Benedict Venetz, their messenger, had a happy knack of falling asleep at every conceivable opportunity. Standing or lying, on grassy knoll or rock pinnacle, it made no difference, Benedict could sleep anywhere for any length of time; and as Mummery and Burgener approached the hotel it looked so deserted that they began to fear the worst—Benedict had gone to sleep on the job again!

Deep sonorous breathing from the hotel lounge confirmed what they suspected and it was a wrathful pair of climbers who prodded the unfortunate Venetz awake. Rubbing the sleep from his eyes, the young man expressed surprise at seeing them. No, lunch was not ready. No, he had not bothered to order it, for he thought the Col du Lion climb was impossible and so they wouldn't turn up anyway! Furthermore, since it seemed likely that he would have to lead a search party to look for them that night, he thought it best to snatch a few moments' sleep!

Such a glib explanation from anybody but Venetz would have brought a sharp retort from Mummery, followed by instant dismissal and goodness knows what curses Alexander would have invoked on the miscreant; but with Benedict they could never be really angry. A neighbour of Burgener's from Stalden, Venetz had an air of injured innocence which appealed to Mummery's sense of humour, and he was looked upon as a sort of court jester. But Mummery was no fool; he also knew that little Venetz was the best rock-climber in the Alps.

After their conquest of the Col du Lion, Mummery and his guides departed from Chamonix, leaving behind them one last great problem on the Matterhorn. This was the Furggen ridge: the only one of the four Matterhorn ridges still unclimbed. Burgener in particular was anxious to have a go at it and so, as soon as they had climbed the Charmoz, which we shall read about in the next chapter, they returned to Zermatt intent on conquering the Furggen.

One of the particular attractions of the Matterhorn, from a climber's point of view, is that each of the four great ridges is quite different from the others. The Hörnli is an easy-angled rock arête, the Italian is a series of towers, the Zmutt has its graceful snow crest and the Furggen rises in enormous steps. One thing they all share in common—the final few hundred feet are much steeper than the rest, and the Furggen is steepest of all.

After a somewhat hectic journey from Chamonix, the three men reached Stalden, where the Saas and Zermatt valleys separate, and there rested for the night. It was a convenient halting place—handy for Burgener's and Venetz's homes—and it allowed the guides to visit their local church so that they could pray for safety on the forthcoming expedition. Mummery, who had little time for religion, tended to scoff at their devotions, but Alexander took a more practical view. As a good Catholic he lit candles to ensure his safety. "One never knows," he hinted darkly, and added with typical peasant shrewdness, "and anyway, it only costs a few francs!"

Next day they continued their journey up the valley to Zermatt and that same evening set off for the Matterhorn. But such continuous effort brought no reward: by the time they reached the Schwartzee, Burgener was feeling distinctly ill and the expedition was postponed.

By the next evening, however, Burgener had recovered sufficiently to start once more up the familiar path to the mountain. As they climbed up the steep track in the darkness they observed a pinpoint of light wandering back and forth across the distant Gorner Glacier. Mummery guessed it to be a lantern (it was actually a guide looking for a party who had lost themselves on the glacier), but his two companions saw in the light something much more sinister—*geister*. Ghosts!

The incident might have passed without much more ado had it not been for the fact that as they reached the boggy ground round the Schwartzee they were surrounded by will o' the wisps, those strange unearthly blue flickerings caused by escaping marsh gas. This was altogether too much for the superstitious guides: they stopped in terror.

Mummery realised at once that he had a crisis on his hands. The two guides really did believe in ghosts, in common with all the valley peasants of that time, and seeing one was a serious matter, for it was a signal of impending doom. The expedition was in danger of foundering.

"You do not understand, mein Herr," cried the frightened Burgener as Mummery sought to convince them otherwise, "anyone who sees a *geist* will die within twenty-four hours."

"In that case," Mummery retorted, "we might as well continue. For if it *is* ghosts we have seen, we shall die anyway, and if it is not, then we've nothing to fear."

But the logic of this reasoning was lost on the men. Mummery, however, had not been Burgener's companion for two years for nothing. He knew the measure of his man and he always managed to play on his weaknesses. Unable to convince him by scientific reasoning, Mummery turned to guile.

"Look at it this way," Mummery said slyly, "since we are to die, would you rather die climbing the mountain or would you rather the Devil came for you in front of all the men of Zermatt?"

It did the trick. As Mummery had hoped, Burgener and Venetz would rather die anywhere than give the satisfaction of such a sight to their Zermatt rivals. The expedition continued.

But they were not finished with apparitions by any means. No sooner had they started than lights appeared on the Hörnli ridge in front of them and it was only when they yodelled and the voice of Young Peter Taugwalder came floating back that they realised the ghosts were just other climbers like themselves.

Once more reassured, they were just continuing on their way when a ghastly apparition sprang out on to the path in front of them to vanish almost immediately. Even Mummery was shaken this time and as for the men they didn't stop to find out what it was, but ran pell-mell for the sanctuary of the nearby Schwartzee chapel!

And it was the chapel which provided the answer. A candle had been left burning on the altar by Taugwalder, and the chapel door, unlatched, was gently swinging in the breeze, alternately throwing out patches of light.

Leaving Burgener and Venetz to their devotions, Mummery went on alone to the Furggen Glacier, hoping that they had seen enough ghosts for one night.

Whether it was that his mind was still on ghosts instead of the job in hand, Burgener tackled the approach to the Furggen ridge in the wrong way, and the party were led into some desperate climbing before they eventually came to the correct couloir. Even then, things did not look too good. The couloir, like so many on the Matterhorn, was obviously a stone-fall danger spot and only the knowledge that the sun was not yet on the upper rocks led them to use it. Once more racing against time, they climbed furiously towards the ridge.

When they had reached the safety of the open ridge they stopped for breakfast, panting violently from so much high-altitude exertion. So busy had they been, in fact, that a change in weather had gone unnoticed, but now they could see that the mountain was surrounded by boiling cumulus which wreathed the upper crags in veils of mist.

The wind was rising too, and as they scrambled up the first easy rocks of their arête, Mummery was filled with foreboding about the prospects of success.

One look at the final towering wall—five hundred feet of almost overhanging rock—convinced him that to try to climb it would be madness. Under good conditions it might be possible, though it would give a severe struggle, but in the present circumstances it was hopeless.

But they could not go back the way they had come because the couloir would by now be too dangerous. Once more the Matterhorn had trapped them.

When climbers find themselves in Mummery's unenviable position—unable to go up or down—they seek a last alternative, an escape to one side or the other, hoping to meet an easier route. It is known as *traversing off*, but, of course, it is not always possible—sometimes the traverse is even more difficult than the climb itself. The question facing Mummery was just that—was it possible to traverse off?

There was only one way they could go: across the upper part of the East Face, just below the final wall, until they met the ordinary route on the Hörnli ridge at the point known as the Shoulder.

Only their extreme predicament could have tempted them into such a traverse. As they grappled with steep rocks, moving foot by foot on small holds, the wind shrieked round their ears, stinging their faces with flying icicles torn from the mountain. All the time stones hummed past their heads or ricocheted off the surrounding rocks.

After a while they were able to shelter on a ledge protected by an overhanging eave of rock, where Burgener insisted that they should eat the rest of their provisions, knowing full well that they would need every ounce of strength to complete the traverse.

Then once more they launched out on to the hair-raising slabs, almost dancing from toehold to toehold, with the stones whistling all round and Burgener roaring into the teeth of the gale, "Schnell! nur Schnell!"

Within a few minutes they were safe from further stonefall, and though the rest of the traverse was difficult they soon reached the security of the Hörnli Shoulder.

After a short rest to recover from the excitements of the day, they hurried up the ordinary route to the summit of the Matterhorn and returned to Zermatt just in time for their evening meal.

Mummery never returned to the Furggen ridge. Though in later years several great mountaineers tried it, the ridge was not climbed until 1911, when three Italians succeeded in avoiding the last great bastion. It was not climbed directly until 1941, and it remains to this day one of the most difficult ridge-climbs in the Alps.

CHAPTER FOUR

GRÉPON

By THE START of the 1880 season very few of the major summits around Chamonix remained unclimbed. One by one, as climbers increased in skill and daring, the great aiguilles had been conquered during the preceding decades. The Plan, Moine, Leschaux, Rochefort, Blaitière, Triolet—these had all been conquered by 1875 and were quickly followed in the next five years by the Droites, Courtes, Noire, Talèfre and finally the Grand and Petit Drus. A host of lesser pinnacles, some as yet unnamed, still remained for future generations to try their skill upon, but of the really big aiguilles only a very small handful remained.

They had all been attempted, naturally enough, and none more often than that pinnacled ridge which forms such a splendid view from the valley, and such an obvious challenge—the Aiguilles des Grands Charmoz. So long as the Charmoz remained unclimbed, no true mountaineer could even look out of his bedroom window at Chamonix without feeling a sense of defiance on the part of the mountains.

The Charmoz rises like a savage granite stickleback from just above the tree line at the Plan de Blaitière and runs southwards until it meets the Col des Nantillons. On the west side it is flanked by the heavily crevassed Glacier des Nantillons, on the other it plummets sheer to the Mer de Glace. The principal summits of this sharp ridge nowadays have names of their own. It begins with the Point Albert, the Aiguille de l'M and the Petit Charmoz—three minor summits scarcely worth bothering about in the old days—then it rises to the Grand Charmoz with its five separate pinnacles, drops again to the head of the Charmoz-Grépon couloir and finally rises to the highest summit of all, the Grépon. From the top of the Grépon it descends to the Col des Nantillons.

In 1880 all this was called simply the Aiguilles des Grands Charmoz, and early attempts on the Charmoz were, in fact, usually attempts on what we now call the Grépon.

They had started nine years earlier and had gone on at fairly regular intervals ever since. Almost every climber of conse-

quence had had a go—from Leslie Stephen down to Clinton
Dent, and Davidson. Usually the climbers tried it from near
the Col des Nantillons—certainly the most obvious looking
route—but they invariably came to a halt at a prominent ledge
known as the C.P. Platform, from two initials some earlier
explorers had painted there.

Mummery's attempt on the mountain was completely fortuitous. After climbing the Col du Lion, he, Burgener and Venetz
journeyed to Courmayeur with the intention of climbing on the
Italian side of Mont Blanc, but the weather turned bad and so,
a few days later, they crossed the Col du Géant to Chamonix.

On the evening of July 14th, the weather having improved,
they set out by lantern-light through the dark pine forests
which clothe the steep sides of the valley, to the Plan des
Blaitière. Their intention was to ascend the northern summit of
the Grands Charmoz, not only because the peak was worth
ascending for its own sake and nobody had yet tried to do so,
but also because it might show them more of the higher summit
—the Grépon.

In the early light they climbed the Nantillons Glacier and
made a hurried crossing below the seracs which threaten this
route, to the foot of the conspicuous Charmoz-Grépon couloir.

This couloir is a very wide, conspicuous rift between the
Charmoz, on its left, and the Grépon on its right. It is also
fairly easy to climb, and the surprising thing is that Mummery
did not follow it as a sure way up to the Charmoz-Grépon ridge,
for he knew that Davidson had ascended it two years earlier
when making an attempt on the Grépon.

However, they had no truck with the tempting couloir.
Instead, they bore away to their left on a line Burgener had
once followed with Dent, over simple slabs and ledges until at
last they were beneath the final cliffs. Here it was deemed
prudent to make a cache of their extra gear, even to the extent
of leaving behind their coats and boots so as to be freer to
engage in difficult rock-climbing. Where Mummery first learnt
this trick of discarding his boots for difficult climbs (a device
often used in later years by rock-climbers in Britain) is not at all
certain: perhaps he invented it, or perhaps it was the invention
of young Venetz, an outstanding climber of difficult rock. In
any event, Venetz took the lead from this point of the climb.

They made their way up the cliff until brought to a halt by
a formidable ice-coated chimney some forty feet high, formed

THE RANGE OF MONT BLANC.

AIG DU TOUR
ORSIÈRES
AIG DU CHARDONNET
Col du Chardonnet
AIG D'ARGENTIÈRE
ARGENTIÈRE
AIG DU CHARDONNET
AIG VERTE
LES DROITES
AIG DE TRIOLET
Col du Dolent
MT. DOLENT
Montenvers
MER DE GLACE
AIG DRU
AIG DU MOINE
Couvercle
AIG DE TALÈFRE
Col de Talèfre
Col de Triolet
CHAMONIX
CHARMOZ
GRÉPON
AIG DU PLAN
AIG DU TACUL
AIG DE ROCHEFORT
GRANDES
JORASSES
AIG DU MIDI
DENT DU REQUIN
AIG GÉANT
MT. MAUDIT
MONT BLANC
MT. BLANC DE COURMAYEUR
AIG DE BIONNASSAY
AIG DE TRÉLATÊTE
Entrèves

by a huge block which had split away from the mountain. Here
the climbing began in earnest. At fifteen feet the ice bulged
out in an ugly fashion, and there were no holds of any sort.

Quite undeterred by its ugly look Venetz climbed into the
icy chimney, Burgener following immediately behind. Mummery, unroped, was left at the foot to await the success or
otherwise of the guides.

By patient wriggling on almost invisible projections of ice,
Venetz managed to draw level with the bulge, being supported
in a most precarious manner by Burgener, who, straddling the
chimney on tiny nicks he had cut in the ice, applied the head
of his axe to his companion's trouser seat. But little Venetz was
not tall enough to see over the bulge. Calmly he requested that
Burgener remove the axe and push it under his feet instead, so
that he might gain a few inches of height. This Alexander did,
whilst Venetz, incredibly, hung from the slippery ice by his
finger-tips!

The antics of his guides made Mummery's heart beat faster
and he was more than thankful when at last they surmounted the
obstacle and dropped the rope-end down so that he could follow.

It was not Mummery's usual habit to carry a knapsack when
climbing, but on this occasion he had taken the load so that his
guides would be unhampered in the climbing and now it
proved a considerable nuisance. It irritated him, threw him off
balance. At the difficult ice bulge he slipped and fell, dangling
like a puppet on the end of the rope. When he felt the jerk,
Burgener peered over at his helpless employer. "Why don't
you come on?" he asked, grinning.

It was probably the only occasion Mummery came off whilst
rock-climbing, and it injured his sense of pride. He privately
considered himself to be in the same class as Burgener and
Venetz, and so he was, though he would have modestly denied
it had anyone asked him directly. However, writing about his
successful Grépon climb some time later he said, "M. Dunod
heard at Chamonix that I took three ladders of ten feet each
on this ascent . . . it led him to encumber himself with three
ladders of *twelve* feet each." Typical of Mummery's sly sense of
humour, the remark nevertheless shows clearly enough that he
knew he was a better rock-climber than most. No wonder he
was mortified at having fallen off where Venetz and Burgener
succeeded! Sensitive as always he referred to himself as
"baggage" and the "despised Herr" for the rest of the climb.

Nevertheless, the despised Herr committed no further *faux-pas*
and at 11.45 a.m. they stood on the summit of the Grands
Charmoz. They had climbed it at the first attempt without any
previous reconnaissance, and it had taken them just three hours
from the foot of the couloir.

After their unsuccessful attempt on the Furggen ridge of the
Matterhorn, Mummery and his guides returned yet again to
Chamonix. With the ascent of the Grands Charmoz still fresh
in their memories, it might be natural to presume that their
intentions were to finish off this ridge by climbing to the highest
point—the Grépon—but such was not the case. In the first
place what they had seen of the Grépon ridge from the Charmoz
had convinced them that there was no possibility of climbing it
from that direction, and in the second place, they had new and
bigger fish to fry.

Their sights were set on the highest, and in many ways, the
most impressive, of the Chamonix peaks still awaiting a first
ascent—the Aiguille du Géant. More remote than the Grépon,
and five hundred metres higher, the imposing granite obelisk of
the Géant had been an early target for the second generation of
climbers. As long before as 1872, both Whitwell and Kennedy
had made attempts on it, and the French climber Charlet had
made an outstanding solo attempt in 1876. A year later Lord
Wentworth and de Filippi tried to climb it by firing rockets, to
which a rope was attached, over the top from a convenient
platform—but all these attempts came to nothing.

The main trouble was that the Géant is much steeper than the
average mountain, steeper even than most of the aiguilles, and
not only that but also very smooth, with small holds and
tremendous exposure. Considering the inadequate safety
precautions which climbers used in those days, it is little wonder
they found the Géant a somewhat nerve-racking climb!

The peak is very like a tower with three faces. The S.E. face
is almost perpendicular throughout its height, overhanging in
places, and is an extremely difficult climb even today, using
modern equipment: quite beyond the pioneers. The north face,
on the other hand, seems fairly straightforward and was the
way most favoured by the early climbers, though it tempts only
to disappoint, as they eventually discovered, for it too is
difficult in its last few hundred feet. Only the S.W. face held out
real chance of success for a first ascent.

In late July, Mummery and Burgener (and possibly Venetz, though we can't be certain) made two attempts on this formidable aiguille. At first they seem to have tried the obvious north face, but not meeting with much success they diverted their attention to the S.W. face. They climbed to within twenty or thirty metres of the summit, or so they thought at the time, and then, unable to go any higher, they built a small cairn on a ledge to mark their highest point. At the foot of the mountain Mummery also left a visiting card in a safe place for whosoever might follow in their footsteps. After noting his highest point, he added cryptically, "Absolutely inaccessible by fair means."

Perhaps it was his conviction that the Géant could not be climbed without artificial aid which prompted Mummery never to return, and later events proved him right. When the Italian brothers Sella reached the summit ridge two years later, their guides—the Macquignaz of Valtournanche—fixed iron spikes and permanent ropes over all the difficult parts. This was not Mummery's idea of climbing at all! Ironically, though, despite their elaborate aids the Sellas did not reach the actual summit of the Géant. The prize was snatched a few days later by an Englishman, W. W. Graham, using the fixed ropes and spikes left behind by the Italians.

When Mummery returned home after his successful season of 1880 he was somewhat surprised to receive a letter from the Editor of the *Alpine Journal* requesting details of his climbs. After his shabby treatment over his election, it must have seemed ironical to Mummery that the Alpine Club was still interested in his adventures, and his reply was guarded.

"I am much too fond of climbing to think it any trouble to write about my scrambles," he replied. "My only regret is that the peculiar position in which I am placed prevents my fully satisfying your wishes."

He meant by this that as a person who had been rejected by the Club he could not see his way to giving a lecture on his climbs to the members, or contributing an article to the journal. As a compromise, however, he included in his letter the brief outline of his climbs on the Matterhorn and Charmoz, and these duly appeared in print as a sort of "news item".

The Aiguille Verte, climbed from the Charpoua Glacier by a route called the Couloir en Y from its obvious shape, was Mummery's opening shot in his 1881 campaign. As a climb it

was difficult, but not a really good route, and notable only for
the fact that Alexander succeeded in breaking his ice-axe yet
again. Nevertheless, they enjoyed themselves, and poor little
Venetz, who had been too indisposed to accompany them on
the expedition was green with envy. Mummery promised him
all the climbing he wanted on the Grépon!

You will remember that on the west side of the Charmoz-
Grépon ridge lies the small but steep Glacier des Nantillons,
while on the east of it is the immense stretch of the Mer de
Glace. It was from the Nantillons that Mummery had ascended
the Charmoz in the previous year, and what he had seen of the
Grépon on that side led him to believe that the Mer de Glace
face might be easier.

Accordingly, Mummery, Burgener and Venetz left the
Montenvers Hotel at 2 a.m. on August 1st, and picking their
way through the stones and crevasses of the Mer de Glace
turned the end of the Trélaporte ridge until, by working left
over the little Trélaporte glacier, they were directly beneath the
Grépon face.

Their intention was to ascend the centre one of three big
couloirs, but finding this impracticable they turned instead to
the one on the left. At first they had considerable difficulty in
crossing the bergschrund but, once across it, easier climbing led
them for several hundred feet up the face. A gully followed this,
after which they were forced out again to the left over a delicate
slab until again they could go more easily upwards.

After eight hours of steady climbing they reached the top of
a prominent red tower and it was obvious that despite all their
efforts there was still a very long way to go to reach the summit
of the Grépon. Moreover, the climbing up ahead looked distinctly difficult. Either they would have to bivouac for the
night, without adequate provisions, or they would have to
retreat. They chose the latter.

Mummery realised from this attempt that the Mer de Glace
face of the Grépon was much more difficult than he had
imagined. It was not climbed until thirty years later.

Now that they knew that the Mer de Glace face was too
difficult they could concentrate their energies on the Nantillons
side. After all, this side of the mountain only *seemed* difficult—
they had not actually put it to the test.

In the early morning of August 3rd they made their way out
of Chamonix and after hours of steady but steep trudging

through the forest paths, reached the Glacier des Nantillons.

This glacier was always a bugbear to Alexander, for he never seemed to pick the right way through its many intricacies. When they climbed the Charmoz he had taken a poor line over the ice, and now again, though he chose a different route, it was scarcely better. They found themselves involved in a long, tedious bout of step-cutting, which was bad enough in itself, but made infinitely worse by the fact that another party, climbing by the correct route, was steadily overhauling them! This made Alexander furious and he redoubled his efforts to race the interlopers on to the upper glacier.

It turned out a dead heat, much to Burgener's chagrin, especially as the other party was led by a well-known guide from the Oberland. Together the two groups went as far as the foot of the Charmoz-Grépon couloir where they parted company. The Oberlander wished Burgener well, but advised him not to try the Grépon. "I have tried it," he said, "and where I have failed no one else need hope to succeed." This was altogether too much for Alexander! He swore loud and long that come what may he would climb the Grépon or die in the attempt. No Oberlander was going to tell *him* what could or could not be done!

After a pause for second breakfast, the trio scrambled unroped up the couloir, looking for some sort of break in the vertical walls guarding the Grépon. About seventy foot below the col they found a slab which seemed to offer them a chance of success, but though Burgener and Mummery both had a try they found that the temptingly easy ground above the slab remained just out of reach.

Meanwhile, Venetz, who had scrambled farther up the gully, shouted that he had discovered a way.

Leaving Alexander to fetch up the rope and knapsack, Mummery hurried to join Venetz. When he arrived at the top of the couloir he could see that the guide was studying a promising slab which leant against the cliffs of the Grépon. The slab itself was smooth and unclimbable, but its edge formed a sort of flake crack with the mountain, which if it could be climbed led to an easy gully topped by a chockstone, beneath which there was a hole on the very crest of the ridge. The crack would at least get them on to the ridge proper—what followed after was a matter of chance.

Burgener joined the party and Venetz, now roped, started on

the crack. In places it was so holdless that he was forced out on
to the slab; nowhere did it admit more than an arm and a leg
at one time. His companions watched, hardly daring to breathe,
as the little guide squirmed and wriggled his way up the fissure,
until at last he could grasp a chockstone, jammed about half-
way up, which helped his progress. Above the chockstone the
crack seemed more difficult still, but the agile guide never
faltered, and finding some hidden holds soon reached the
top.

As Mummery followed, held on the rope, he found the crack
exceedingly difficult and he wondered how Venetz, whose
reach was at least a foot less than his own, had managed to lead
it. Later on, when the route became widely known, climbers
spoke of reaching the Grépon by "Mr. Mummery's crack"
which in the course of time became shortened to "the Mummery Crack": almost certainly the most famous single pitch in
the Alps.

Once they had climbed the crack they went up easy rocks in
the gully above, then through the hole in the ridge, called by
Burgener "Kanones Loch" because it looked to him as though
the ridge had been shot through by a cannon ball. From here
they could look straight down at the Mer de Glace, thousands
of feet below. They had passed from one side to the other, clear
through the mountain!

Fortified by a drink of Bouvier they returned to the attack. A
stiff little chimney with a capstone led them back to the
Nantillons face of the ridge again where they came across a
curious slanting flake which could only be climbed à cheval, that
is, by sitting astride it and squirming up. The flake was sharp
and painful, but what bothered Alexander was the fact that
such a jogging procedure might break the remaining wine
bottles—a disaster too horrible to contemplate!

Beyond the flake, now called the "Râteau de Chèvre"
(though it would be an unusual nanny-goat that came this
way!) they arrived without further difficulty at the pinnacle
marking the summit of the Grépon. Once again they had
succeeded at a first attempt.

They returned to Chamonix content in the knowledge that
the Grépon had been conquered; but that night Mummery's
mind, thinking over the events and scenes of the day's adventure, began to be assailed by doubt. The Grépon has two
summits, north and south, and though the northern one, which

they had just climbed, seemed at first to be the higher, on reflection Mummery was not so sure. He determined to go back and find out.

So it was that two days later, on August 5th, the same trio repeated their ascent as far as the north summit, then continued along the ridge to the south.

The climbing was easier than they had expected. They negotiated a gap by sliding down a knotted rope and before long found themselves on a curious flat ledge on the Mer de Glace face, along which they were able to walk quite comfortably—indeed, Mummery later described it as being "suitable for carriages, bicycles, or other similar conveyances", and it has been known ever since as the "Vire aux Bicyclettes".

But if the route to the southern summit was without much difficulty, the peak itself looked a formidable proposition. Smooth to the touch, vertical and topped by an overhanging capstone, it seemed truly unassailable. Only one way offered any chance at all: a wide crack, absolutely smooth, devoid even of chockstones, split the block from top to bottom.

About six feet above the gap from which the pinnacle rises there is a narrow ledge formed by the spine of the ridge. Mummery's quick eye for protection saw at once that it might be possible for a man standing on this ledge to throw a rope over the top of the pinnacle, and so aid the leader in making his ascent of the desperate crack.

It was a good plan, though perhaps not quite playing the game, but unfortunately neither he nor Burgener could get the rope to land across the gendarme. In the end, frustrated by their efforts, they decided that it was cheating and that the crack would have to be climbed legitimately.

Whilst his companions were amusing themselves with rope-tricks, Benedict Venetz had seized the opportunity to have a nap. Now he was rudely awakened by the insistent prodding of an ice-axe, informed of the good news about their failure to secure a top rope, and told to get started.

Mummery had, as usual, worked out a plan to help Venetz as much as possible. It was simply this: he would stay at the foot of the crack and help him up it by pushing and holding his feet in place as high as he could, and then Alexander, stationed on the rock ledge six feet higher would render further assistance from there. What the young guide thought of all this is hard to say, but Venetz was not the complaining sort: a crack was just a crack to him and if Herr Mummery said climb it, then climb it he must—that's what he was paid to do.

With Mummery's aid he lodged himself in the crack and started to climb. At first he could use his employer's shoulder and hands to steady himself, and then Burgener leant over from his perch and jammed his axe across the crack, which helped even further. Soon, however, Venetz was beyond reach, fighting the crack on his own.

His companions were once more held breathless by the young guide's extraordinary skill. Inch by inch he worked his way up the smooth crack, pausing now and then for breath, apparently unconcerned at the terrifying space below him. At last he neared the top. This was the crux, for tired through struggling up the holdless crack, Venetz had now to pull over on to the summit capstone. One hand reached over and found a sharp edge, then the other, and quickly, before the blood ran out of his arms, he gave a mighty heave. He was up!

At once the two watchers, their tension relieved, gave yells of delight. It was Venetz's finest hour, for now truly was the Grépon conquered.

CHAPTER FIVE

INTERLUDE

Upon his return from the Alps in 1881 Mummery resumed his correspondence with the editor of the *Alpine Journal*, who was still pressing him for an article. The Rev. W. A. B. Coolidge was not a man to be easily put off; a forthright American who had made his home in England, he was not only a keen mountaineer but a walking encyclopaedia of Alpine knowledge. It is doubtful if anyone has ever equalled, much less surpassed, the accumulated store of Alpine information which this strange fanatic possessed, and he was an obvious choice as journal editor. Nothing missed his keen eye, nobody was too important or too obscure to badger, if they could contribute to the sum of Alpine experience.

Mummery, however, hung back, even when Coolidge dangled before him the tempting carrot of A.C. election again.

"I thank you heartily for your kind offer to attempt to 'run' me again for the A.C.," Mummery wrote, "but I do not care to risk a second defeat.

"It does not seem to be desirable for those who are not members of the Club to send notes to the A.J. but if you would really like to make any extracts from this letter, pray do so."

He then went on to describe in some detail his ascents of the Verte and the Charmoz, but his excuse for not writing an article was merely an evasion, and Coolidge knew it. After all, Mummery had contributed an article in 1880, after his ascent of the Zmutt arête, when he thought he would be elected.

A month later he wrote again. "If you think it desirable I will (presuming you can give me the assurance suggested in one of your letters) put up again for the A.C. I do not see any other way in which I could become a contributor to the A.J. without exposing myself to unpleasing comments."

This sounds uncommonly like a little bit of gentle pressure being exerted on Coolidge—a sort of counter-carrot—but Coolidge realised that Mummery was in earnest. He also realised that he had promised more than he could fulfil.

He did not reply, but like Brer Rabbit, he just waited. Sure

enough, Mummery, who was no match for the wily editor at
this sort of game, wrote again, revealing his anxiety:

"I take it I am right in assuming from your silence, that on
second thoughts you agree with me in thinking it undesirable
for me again to seek election to the English A.C.?

"I am sorry to trouble you any more about this matter, but
for one or two reasons I should like to know your own and the
feelings of the A.C. on the subject."

Coolidge now began a tactical retreat. He wrote a detailed
letter explaining that if the matter were in his hands alone,
nothing would give him greater pleasure than to see Mummery
elected (and this was probably true at the time), but as things
stood, there were certain difficulties. . . .

Again Mummery felt the sour taste of disappointment and his
letter in reply was pathetically bitter.

"Personally, I am conceited enough to think that I can do
quite as well without the A.C. as the A.C. can do without me."
And later the astounding charge that, "a well-known member
of your club and a nominal supporter of my last candidature,
made tempting offers to my guide, both in money and employ-
ment, if he would make the expedition to fail." Mummery
meant Davidson, of course, though he did not name him and
marked the letter "private"! Note the bitterness of "your
club" and the derogatory use of the small "c"! He did not
contribute to the journal, and in fact it was ten years before his
account of the Charmoz and Grépon climbs appeared in
print.

He was now feeling very bitter about the whole question of
his acceptance by the "official" Alpine world. What more
could he do to show them that not only was he worthy of
membership, but one of the finest mountaineers of his day?
Had he not served his apprenticeship for longer than most, and
then conquered new and formidable routes which were as
difficult as anything climbed previously?

Matters came to a head with the publication of the Novem-
ber issue of the *Alpine Journal*, 1882. In it was an article by
Alessandro Sella, recent conqueror of the Aiguille du Géant, in
which the second paragraph commented on Mummery's
attempt.

"The difficulties begin at the point at which Mr. Mummery
stopped," wrote Sella, "and which is about a hundred metres
from the Summit, and not twenty or thirty metres as this

gentleman says on a visiting card which I found at the foot of the Dent."

Mummery was furious. From the tone of the paragraph he felt that Sella was accusing him of lying, of claiming more than he had actually achieved. Moreover, since the *Alpine Journal* had printed it without question, without even asking his opinion, Mummery felt that Coolidge supported Sella's remarks. He demanded a printed apology, did not get one, and so ceased all further communication with Coolidge.

The whole affair was really quite stupid and petty, for though practically every climber read the *Alpine Journal*, none thought any the worse of Mummery for Sella's remarks—indeed, most mountaineers were so shocked at the way Sella had ascended the Géant by elaborate spikes and fixed ropes, that any comment he made about other people was ignored. Perhaps Coolidge was a little tactless in printing Sella's article without first referring it to Mummery, but then, that was typical Coolidge— a man not exactly noted for tact, one who had at various times fallen out with almost every climber in the country. That Mummery should take the business so much to heart shows how sensitive he was to the opinions of his fellow mountaineers at this time.

Indeed, it was almost the last straw as far as Mummery was concerned. Everything in the Alpine world seemed to militate against him—accused of bad manners in "stealing" the Zmutt ridge from Penhall, blackballed out of the Alpine Club, accused of lying about the Géant—added together these came to within an ace of breaking his pride. Then, too, despite his spectacular successes on the Matterhorn and the Grépon, his victories had been hard won against physical handicaps which would have stopped men of lesser spirit.

Was it all worth it? Was it worth while having one's character dragged in the mud and enduring pain and discomfort for the sake of a few mountain peaks? Mummery had growing doubts and suddenly, in 1882, like a light extinguished, he stopped climbing.

For four years he retired completely from the world of aiguilles and seracs which he had dominated so well. His gaunt figure, which always seemed as though it was on the point of starvation, and his pinched, bespectacled face with its sharp eyes, were missing from the familiar rounds of Zermatt and Chamonix. Other climbers wondered at his absence, then

forgot. He was not one of them, he had always been something
of a lone wolf: brilliant, no doubt, but a shooting star, and
shooting stars never last long.

Mummery's "lost years" have remained a tantalising puzzle
for Alpine historians. When he wrote his adventures in *My
Climbs* some years later, he made no mention of anything that
happened between 1881 and 1887, and though scholars have
done much patient research they have met with scant success.
Unfortunately, the family papers were destroyed in an air raid
during the last war, before anyone examined them properly,
and some of his notes which came into the possession of the
Alpine Club mysteriously disappeared from the library.
Whether these documents would have told us anything is
impossible to say: they might, for instance, have confirmed that
he spent his summers during the time in question, wandering
in the little-known Maritime Alps and Algeria; two regions he
is known to have visited at some period in his life.

On March 7th, 1883, Mummery married Mary Petherick, a
solicitor's daughter from Exeter. His wife, who was devoted to
him, began to share his love of the mountains. It could well be
that his absence from the limelight during these years was
because he was introducing Mrs. Mummery to easier mountains than those around Chamonix, and that he found in this
something quite new in his experience—a companion who could
share his adventures, someone he could laugh and talk with,
one who would be content just to be with him all the time.

They certainly took an Alpine holiday in 1886, for we know
that the Mummerys crossed the Bietch Pass from Bel Alp to the
Lotchental in the August of that year, and without guides. It
may well have been Mrs. Mummery's first season amongst the
great mountains of the Oberland and the Valais, and one can
imagine with what pride her husband pointed out the peaks he
had climbed, and promised that soon they would climb them
together.

In the following summer they went to the Alps quite early—
in mid-June—where Mary Mummery was introduced to two
of her husband's oldest friends: the kindly, helpful Franz Andermatten, now fifty-three years old, and, of course, the great
Alexander Burgener, about whom she had heard so much. They
were together for a month, during which time they climbed the
Jungfrau, Drieckhorn, Zinal Rothorn, Matterhorn, and the
Täschhorn. Mostly these were done by their ordinary routes,

ut when it came to the Täschhorn, Alexander had something pecial in store. He knew of a ridge which nobody had managed o climb; a fearsome coxcomb of broken rock which earned its iame of "Teufelsgrat"—the Devil's Ridge. Why should they iot all make the first ascent? "Alexander Burgener holds many trange opinions," Mary wrote, "he believes in ghosts, he)elieves also that women can climb!"

She wrote in irony, for in those days women were expected to :now their place, and their place was not the jagged ridge of ome difficult mountain. In exceptional circumstances, if they vere considered strong, and not subject to the vapours or other nysterious feminine ailments, they might be allowed up an :asy snow-peak like the Breithorn, but anything else was inthinkable. A few females had rebelled against this idea but,)y and large, lady climbers were frowned upon.

The Teufelsgrat climb came immediately after the Matter- 1orn, which was the first mountain Burgener and Mrs. Mummery had climbed together. Her performance must have mpressed the guide, or he would not have suggested the Teufelsgrat at all.

The Täschhorn is the second highest of the Mischabel peaks, hat splendid range which separates the Saas and Zermatt valleys. It is a very impressive mountain, whether seen from the Saas side, where it rears up in great walls of red rock, or from :he Zermatt side where its ridges and its triangular summit shows to perfection.

The Teufelsgrat is a long ridge running west-south-west from :he summit, joining the Täschhorn to the smaller peak of the Kinhorn.

On the afternoon of July 15th the Mummerys and their guides, together with some friends, gathered at the old chalets of the Täsch Alp, a delightful valley overlooking the village of Täsch. There was no inn there, in those days, and no climbers' hut on the slopes above the Alp, as there is today, so the party decided to stay the night in one of the hay sheds.

It was a merry gathering. In the afternoon they had a running fight with a cantankerous bull which at one point chased them all on to the roof of the chalet, and that night they enjoyed an evening's music and dancing, with songs from the guides and porters, and thin reedy music from Andermatten's pipes. Certainly none of them cared a fig what the morrow would bring, and both Mummery and Burgener must have

contrasted the gay proceedings with the bitter night they had
spent on the Schönbeil rocks before their attempts on th
Zmutt.

At last they tired of singing and dancing and composed
themselves for sleep, but scarcely had they begun to settle that
the chalet door received a mighty bang, followed by a roar
Their old enemy the bull had come to do battle again! Seizing
the ice-axes and anything else that happened to be convenien
the party rushed out into the night and chased the enraged
animal off down the valley.

There was not much point in going back to sleep after thi
midnight sortie. Instead, they made ready for their departure
and at 1.30 a.m. set off for the Teufelsgrat.

The way up to the Wiengarten Glacier is both steep and
unpleasant, but as the first rays of the morning began to tin
the upper reaches of the mountains they found themselves nea
the foot of their ridge.

Two enormous couloirs split the Teufelsgrat near the poin
where it meets the Kinhorn, offering convenient access to the
ridge. That on the left is obviously a place for stonefall so Bur
gener, with his usual good sense, chose the other. They roped
up, Burgener leading, then Mrs. Mummery, Andermatten and
Mummery last.

Almost at once they came across the curse of the Teufelsgrat
rotten rock. Every hand and foothold had to be tested fo
security, and Alexander, keeping a careful eye on Mrs. Mum
mery would yell from time to time, "You kill your man, you no
like that!" A warning not to kick stones down on her husband
below.

Just when they seemed to be near the crest of the ridge,
Burgener, who was climbing a delicate pitch, let out a groan and
a string of Saastal swear-words which it was fortunate his lady
companion failed to understand. It turned out that a large
stone had moved as he was handling it, crushing his thumb.
"I no more strong in that hand," he moaned, looking at the
bleeding mass. Mummery suggested that they ought to retreat
in the circumstances, but Alexander would have none of it. He
could see how near they were to the ridge, and a half-bottle of
Bouvier soon put him right. He let out a loud yodel and cried
"Forward!" as though about to lead a cavalry charge.

Once they gained the ridge things went well for a time until
Andermatten, now leading, began to tackle a formidable tower.

Charmoz and Grépon Looking back along the narrow crest of the Grépon to the pinnacles of the Charmoz. (*Photo C. D. Milner*)

The Charpoua face of the Aiguille Verte (Photo C. D. Milner)

He inched his way up until he managed to hug the summit block, when, for some inexplicable reason, his arms gave way and he hurtled out into space!

At once, Burgener, who had come up below the tower to assist Andermatten, grabbed the rope, so breaking the fall to some extent. Mummery, as last man, half flung himself over the other side of the ridge the better to hold the party, and his wife grasped at the projecting rock.

Andermatten came to rest some fifteen feet below the ridge on an ice-glazed rock. On examination it was discovered that though he had suffered only a slight head wound, he was badly shaken. Shock had reduced him to a trembling wreck, and for the rest of the expedition he was a constant source of anxiety.

In the meantime, Mummery had checked the knapsack which Andermatten was carrying. "How providential, both bottles of Bouvier are not broken," he remarked, as Andermatten lay gasping on the ground!

Burgener took the lead again, and the luckless Andermatten came last. With both guides injured, the party was now in a dangerous predicament: like a motor-car only firing properly on two cylinders, they could not afford to have anything else go wrong or they would come to a halt.

The ridge turned out to be a mixture of good snow, along which they could fairly race, hard ice which caused endless step cutting, and abominably rotten rock. It was this last which caused them most trouble—they never knew whether they could trust a hold or not, and they were constantly afraid of rocks falling on them from above, for frequently they were not on the crest of the ridge at all, but avoiding obstacles by traverses to one side or another.

Mrs. Mummery lost her ice-axe, but this was a small matter compared with the fact that they were cold and hungry, the time was slipping by, and the weather threatened to become stormy.

To give Alexander a relief, Mummery took over the lead. They traversed the flanks of the ridge until at one point it was obvious that they could go no farther, but must reach the crest again. Under Burgener's direction, Mummery cut steps towards some steep slabs leading to the arête but these proved a false hope—they were too steep and slippery to be climbed. On the immediate flank of the slabs, however, was a narrow ice-filled gully which gave some hope. Mummery led up this until the

c

ice gave out and he was forced to clamber on to some rocks on the right which seemed to offer progress. At once, however, he came to a halt; he could not go forward and it seemed uncertain whether he could get back!

Realising the extreme urgency of the situation, Burgener untied himself from the rope and, using it as a handrail, climbed up until he was level with his employer. Mummery was safe enough, for the time being, so the guide prospected around for a way ahead. Eventually he climbed to the left, nicking small steps in the ice, then, where the gully became shallower, ploughing up through deep powder snow.

Though Burgener had found a way to the ridge he was, of course, unroped, and Mummery now had to follow where the guide had led. He managed it with his usual calm dexterity though it was three-quarters-of-an-hour before the party were once more moving together.

No sooner had they overcome this difficulty than another presented itself. Mummery, who was leading again, called Burgener forward to take a look. "God Almighty, impossible!" cried Burgener.

They seemed to be standing on the edge of the world. In front of them the ridge which they had been following so certainly ended abruptly in a precipice. Its continuation—beyond a quite impossible gap—was a vertical, unclimbable cliff.

As they looked at this formidable obstacle, black despair swept over them. Alexander pronounced it impossible and so it was—only a bird could cross such a gap. Yet to go back was almost equally impossible. They were tired, hungry, dispirited; two members of the party were injured and none of them had had a rest for many hours.

But once the initial shock of meeting the obstacle had worn away, they began to apply common sense to the problem. A great ridge, like the one they were on, simply could not end in mid-air—it was against the laws of nature. Looking about them they found that in fact the "crest" of this arête was really a tremendous overhang of rock, like a fantastic stone leaf jutting out from the main line of the ridge. This meant that the ridge proper was below their jutting perch, and they must get down to it before they could go any farther.

This was easier said than done. The rock was fashioned like loose tiles and the angle was steep. At the bottom it dropped away in a gap to the joint with the main ridge, and anyone who came off whilst trying to cross the gap would pendulum into space. Mummery had to try it—it was their only chance.

He inched down the loose slabs until he came to the gap. Here there was a niche in the rock which would allow the rope to run in the right direction provided it was kept taut. Consequently, the rope was fixed for Mummery to lower himself down and he disappeared from his companion's view. Anxiously they waited, then to their joy he appeared on the other side of the gap. He had made it!

After that, nothing could stop them and at last they could see the final snow slopes of the summit. "The Teufelsgrat is as good as conquered!" cried an exultant Burgener, and indeed it was. At 5.30 p.m. they stood on the summit of the Täschhorn.

Tired and cold though they were they rejoiced in their great victory. It had been hard won against all sorts of misfortune.

They could not stay long, however: the hour was late and a storm was building up. Crashes of thunder rolled round the peaks of the Mischabel as they hurried down the ordinary route on their way back to the glacier. Compared with the ascent it was easy, but Alexander took it at a cracking pace, hustling Mrs. Mummery along. "You must go on," he shouted encouragingly, "I could hold a cow here!"

In the gathering darkness they reached the snout of the glacier, and after an arduous descent of the moraines and pine woods, arrived in the valley at 5.30 a.m. next morning.

The Teufelsgrat had taken twenty-eight hours.

CHAPTER SIX

WIDENING HORIZONS

THROUGH HIS WIFE, Mummery had made a circle of friends and acquaintances in Exeter, three of whom became very close and played a part in his life's story.

The first of these was his brother-in-law, W. J. Petherick, who became his frequent companion in the Alps from 1889 onwards, when together they made the first crossing of the Schreckjoch, without guides, and who was with Mummery on his second Caucasus visit of 1890. Petherick did not aspire to be a great climber, seeming content to tour the various Alpine regions with Mummery and retiring into the background whenever some particularly ambitious expedition was in the offing. Indeed, apart from his tours with his illustrious brother-in-law, Petherick did no climbing at all and he retired from active mountaineering on Mummery's death.

The Pethericks had for several generations been close friends of the Bristows, and Miss Lily Bristow was the particular companion and confidante of Mary Petherick. When Mary married Mummery, Miss Bristow seems to have been caught up in the mountaineering spirit which had infected the Petherick family, and before long she too became an enthusiastic Alpinist. Her skill and daring soon raised her to the forefront of climbing —she made the first *descent* of the Zmutt ridge, and, as we shall see, joined Mummery in some of his best expeditions.

Third of the trio from Exeter was J. A. Hobson, a schoolmaster who collaborated with Mummery in writing *The Physiology of Industry*, published in 1889. Hobson had been much intrigued by some of Mummery's startlingly original ideas concerning economics, and though at first he could not agree with them, Mummery's persuasion gradually convinced him that the ideas were sound. For a few years they worked together on these theories and the book was a formal presentation of their case. It was not, however, the end of Mummery's interest in economic questions—from this time onwards he became more and more involved in theories of political economy and at the time of his death he was seriously considering retiring from his tannery business in order to devote all his time to them.

On these three people, as on his later climbing companions Mummery had a tremendous impact. His boundless energy, his wit, his outstanding intellectual gifts—these all added up to the sort of genius that makes a man a natural leader, whom others follow as a matter of course. Lord Conway, himself a noted mountaineer, said of him: "Never was there a more generous man nor one freer from cant . . . unusually intelligent and gifted . . . not a mere climber. He was full of interest in interesting things. He was intellectually rather than aesthetically endowed. His mind was philosophical and at home in the abstract. Problems of political economy were specially attractive to him. He approached such questions with the same freedom from prejudice, the same original unfettered freshness of mind, with which he approached a mountain."

This freshness of mind, as Conway calls it, had already turned Mummery's thoughts towards the ultimate mountains: the Himalaya. Several times he had thought of visiting these distant ranges, then virtually unknown to mountaineers, and he had even gone so far as to plan expeditions, but always something turned up to prevent the fulfilment of his plans. In 1888, however, he did manage to visit the Caucasus, taking with him as guide Heinrich Zurfluh of Meiringen.

Though most of us regard the Alps as the highest mountains in Europe, and Mont Blanc as the highest peak, in the strictest geographical sense this is not the case. The Caucasus Mountains dividing Europe from Asia, are much higher.

The main range of the Caucasus extends from the Black Sea to the Caspian, a distance of some 750 miles. In character they are simpler than the Alps in so far as they form an almost straight line, like an immense wall, though within their own confines there are side valleys and ridges which make for complexities. The chief interest, so far as mountaineers are concerned, is in the central part of this range where the peaks are of solid granite, best rock of all for climbing, and where they are higher than elsewhere. Here, in a district once known as Saunetia, the range divides into two chains for about 125 miles between the great peaks of Elbrus (18,481 ft), the highest of all, and Hasbek (16,558 ft). The southernmost of the two chains is not so high as its northern counterpart, though more continuous. The northern chain, containing giants like Koshtan Tau (16,876 ft) and Dych Tau (17,054 ft), has been subjected over the ages to the rapid cutting back of fiercely eroding rivers

which have tended to separate one group from the next. Thick
pine forests clothe the lower valleys and lead the traveller's
eyes upwards to a region of tortured glaciers and snowfields
on an immense scale, and above them the sharp granitic peaks.
The whole region has a sense of wild grandeur beyond anything
imaginable in the Alps.

Even when the Golden Age of the Alps was still in full swing,
English mountaineers had been attracted to these remote
fastnesses. In 1864, Freshfield, Moore and Tucker climbed
Elbrus and between then and Mummery's visit of 1888, there
had been nine further expeditions by leading members of the
Alpine Club. It showed considerable daring on their part—the
country had been occupied by the Russians against the wishes
of the native Circassians, and guerilla warfare had been going
on between the two sides for years. Though the country was
officially pacified in 1864, the Russo-Turkish War of 1877–78
led to fresh outbreaks of fighting, and well into the present
century the whole region was a notorious place for brigands.
Hardly the sort of area one would choose for a quiet holiday,
but the Victorian mountaineers were a tough breed who
regarded a few brigands merely as an extra excitement well
within the capabilities of an English gentleman.

In point of fact, when Mummery arrived in the area towards
the end of June 1888 he found things much easier than he had
expected. Travel was not difficult, food was easily obtainable,
and the inhabitants, though wild-looking hunters, were very
friendly. The old chieftain who ruled the Bezingi tribe became
especially friendly, and on several occasions Mummery dined
with him in his private appartments: in return, Mummery
made him gifts of tea and sugar which were much appreciated.
Because of his cordial relationship with the chief, Mummery
had no difficulty in hiring a local man to act as porter and he
was very impressed by the way in which this man, and others
he met, could hold their own when it came to travelling over
rough country. On steep rock they were as good as Alpine
guides, though they knew little about ice-craft.

Now, although Mummery was attracted by the unknown
mysteries of the Caucasus, and though he did make several
journeys of exploration, crossing from one valley to the next,
usually by high passes which nobody had previously crossed, he
was not by nature a mountain explorer. "Climbing was what
he enjoyed," said Conway, "not exploring. He cared nothing

about the geography of mountains, and was bored by surveying and photographing instruments. It was the sheer joy of difficult scrambling which possessed him."

He came to the Caucasus, therefore, with very definite intentions of climbing, and because there were some plums just ripe for a man like himself.

At that time, though the highest summit of the area had been climbed (a somewhat laborious snow plod) the next three highest had resisted any attack. Mummery turned his attention to the highest of the three, called Dych Tau (see map, p. 74).

As it turned out, their first attempt came to nothing. Mummery was not fit enough after the enforced idleness of the long journey from England.

Nevertheless, on the very next day, Zurfluh being indisposed, he set out on a lone climb just to "take a look" at the defences of Dych Tau. Wandering round the south side he came across a buttress which seemed almost a separate peak in itself, and having nothing better to do, he climbed it to the top—about 13,500 feet.

It was a daring piece of cragsmanship, one which has scarcely ever been rivalled in country so unknown as the Dych Tau massif then was. His reward was a series of magnificent views westwards across the Bezingi Glacier and the Zanner Pass towards Saunetia and eastwards over the ridge which joins Dych Tau to Shkara towards the mountains at the head of the Cherek valley. Principally, however, his interest was focused on the great south face of Dych Tau itself. He observed that the mountain had twin peaks, rivalling one another in height, and what was of more immediate interest, that the whole face was plastered with fresh snow from recent storms. Any ascent under those conditions might well be impossible—certainly difficult— so he determined to postpone Dych Tau until conditions were more favourable.

The next two weeks he devoted to a circular tour round the adjoining valleys. His first objective was an attempt on Shkara which quickly came to nothing, though in fact Zurfluh had pointed out how it might be climbed by the ridge from Dych Tau—a judgement which was proved correct by later explorers. Mummery, however, feared that the ridge route might be too long, and he chose instead a face route which turned out to be hopelessly crevassed and guarded by immense ice-falls.

Thwarted in his attempts to reach a high summit, Mummery

returned to Kosh in the Bezingi valley, then journeyed over th
Zanner Pass to Mujal in Saunetia where the headman greetec
him with great courtesy and hospitality, despite the fact that h
had a Bezingi porter with him, the Bezingis being traditiona
enemies of the Saunetians.

Two days later Mummery moved on again, this time turning
north to make a hair-raising crossing of the Taibo and Leksu
passes to the Chegem valley. On this journey he was mucl
impressed by the beautiful great obelisk of Ushba (15,409 ft)
perhaps the finest of all the Caucasian mountains. It is just the
sort of mountain that would attract Mummery: a veritable
Matterhorn of a peak, with twin summits and a west face
6,000 feet high, but for some reason the Englishman chose tc
ignore it. Like Shkara, Ushba was climbed later in the same
year by J. G. Cockin and the Swiss guide Ulrich Almer.

From the Chegem valley, Mummery turned south and east
again to make his way back to Bezingi. He judged the time was
right to attempt Dych Tau. Zurfluh, too, was anxious to make
the ascent, but for a very different reason. Away from his
native Alps the guide felt ill at ease, and suffered from bouts of
depression, or to put it more simply, he was homesick! He was
no fit companion for a man of Mummery's temperament, and
many a time the Englishman must have wished devoutly that
he had brought Burgener instead.

Though the weather was by no means perfect, Mummery and
Zurfluh, with the aid of a Bezingi shepherd, set up their tent as
high as they could below the mountain, and at about 2.30 a.m.,
next morning, July 24th, began their ascent. They aimed first
of all at the col which lay between the buttress Mummery had
previously climbed and the main mass of Dych Tau: then,
having reached this without any difficulty, they turned to their
right, making for a long prominent couloir which seams this
side of the mountain.

The going was easy, but there is an old climber's adage which
says that accidents usually happen in the easy places—and
soon there was a perfect example of this. A mass of hard snow,
struck by Zurfluh's axe, broke away from the slope to go
crashing on to Mummery's skull. Fortunately, the Englishman
was close up behind his guide, so the lump had no time to
gather momentum before it hit him or he would have been
killed. As it was, he was badly concussed and for a minute or
two scarcely knew where he was or what had happened. It took

Victorian climbers below the Requin. (*Photo G. P. Abraham*)

THE GRÉPON TRAVERSE On the left is the Charmoz and the Charmoz–Grépon couloir. The dotted line shows the route to the top and the descent by the C.P. route. (*Photo C. D. Milner*)

him fully five minutes to regain his proper senses, but he insisted on carrying on and gradually the effects of the blow wore off.

When they reached the gully it proved to be steeper and harder than they had expected. Instead of snow, it was hard ice, and a long bout of step-cutting seemed inevitable. Zurfluh, however, had a novel way with ice. Instead of cutting a staircase of steps as was the usual procedure in those days, when climbers did not wear crampons, he would cut steps for his left foot only, and by a sort of mantelshelf action, with his right boot acting as a kind of balance against the intervening ice, leap from one hold to the other. It was certainly a quick way of climbing ice, somewhat similar in principle to a method used by very skilful modern climbers, but Mummery thought it too dangerous by half! Though Zurfluh showed him how it was done he politely declined to try, cutting the intervening steps himself.

They were now fairly on their mountain and soon reached the great subsidiary rib which divides the south face of Dych Tau and leads to the higher of the twin summits. On their left was the big ice couloir they had just quitted, whilst away to the right the face of the peak, plastered with ice and wrinkled with a thousand minor ribs and gullies, stretched away to the next mountain, Mishingi Tau.

The rib went easily enough until eventually they were forced to a halt by an overhang. It was a convenient place to rest and they knew they were not far from the summit, though at the same time they realised that the climbing was becoming more serious. They had a good meal and made a cache of their superfluous gear.

A quick survey to the right of their platform convinced Zurfluh that there was no progress to be had that way, so he led off to the left across a huge slab, balancing like a fly on delicate holds, many of which were ice-coated. Zurfluh, in common with all of Mummery's guides, was a fine rock-climber, and he seemed not to notice the immense drop underneath him. Mummery followed without hesitation.

In a little while they got above the overhang and found themselves on a short, horizontal crest of knife-like sharpness. Beyond, there was a gap, then the final steep rocks to the summit.

Zurfluh pressed on, regardless of both difficulties and

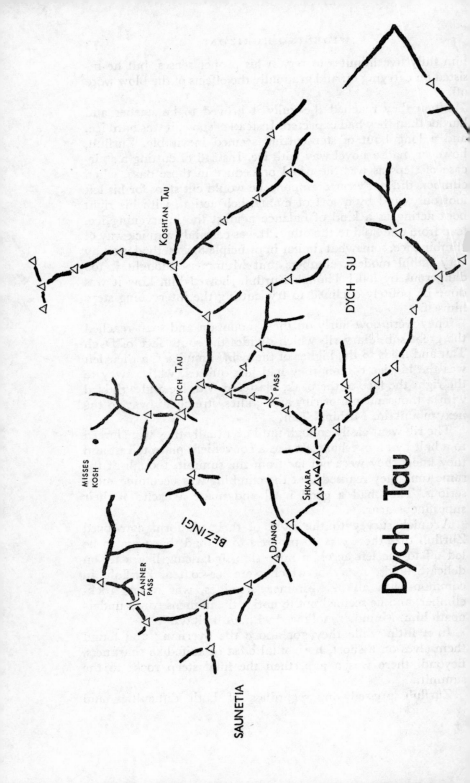

dangers, until at last Mummery cried halt. He pointed out that they were about to make the first ascent of the second highest mountain in all Europe, and that under these circumstances they might be advised to show some respect for the rules of good mountaineering. For example, they could start by putting on the rope!

Incredible though it may seem, both men had *soloed* Dych Tau to within an ace of the top!

When Mummery made his demands, Zurfluh was already above a very nasty-looking wall. He grinned down at his employer. "Shall I drop the rope down to you, or would you prefer to come up for it?" he demanded jokingly.

When Mummery had tied on he noted with relief what an amazing difference it made. Rocks which had seemed vertical and difficult suddenly appeared much easier. He was not the first or the last climber to discover what a difference a "top-rope" makes!

They were now well above the col which separates the two peaks of Dych Tau, and before long a good crack led them easily to the summit.

By 4 p.m. they were back at camp, being congratulated by their guide, the shepherd, who had watched their activities all day. The next morning they packed up and descended the Bezingi valley to Tubeneli where the old chief gave them a great welcome.

Mummery wanted to stay on and make further ascents but, unfortunately, Zurfluh would have none of it. Now that Dych Tau was vanquished he could think of nothing but returning home.

Mummery was well pleased with his summer in the Caucasus. He had climbed the highest unclimbed peak in the area, and thus in Europe, and as he himself said, he had never enjoyed a holiday half so much before. His success attracted considerable attention, and he was invited to read a paper on his Caucasian travels to the Royal Geographical Society.

And so at last he received official recognition. He felt that, socially, events were turning his way and in this he was right. In December 1888, Albert Frederick Mummery was elected a Member of the Alpine Club.

CHAPTER SEVEN

TWO DAYS ON AN ICE-SLOPE

MUMMERY'S ELECTION to the Alpine Club did not mean that all the petty feuds and jealousies of which he had been a victim for so long were dead. There were still those who would rather have had him out than in, though their numbers and influence had waned during the eight years since his first application.

Edward Whymper, conqueror of the Matterhorn, now a middle-aged man with grey hair and a short temper, was one of those who disliked Mummery, being consumed by jealousy at the man's exploits. Whymper doubtless mistook Mummery as a rival for the public's attention, someone whose climbs were so daring that they made his own ascents seem small beer by comparison. He attacked Mummery's method of climbing as foolhardy, and long after the climber was dead, he wrote a slashing, vicious review of *My Climbs*. Even Mummery's obituary in the *Alpine Journal* was not sacred: "His untimely death is a grievous loss to the club," the obituary said. In his precise, pedantic way, the old lion took out his pocket pencil and wrote alongside, in his own copy, "I do not agree".

The Rev. W. A. B. Coolidge once told Sir Arnold Lunn a curious story about Mummery's election. According to Coolidge, he was in charge of the ballot-boxes during the evening in question, and to his dismay he saw that Mummery was going to be blackballed once again. Realising that it would be unthinkable for the Club to reject a man who was rapidly becoming acknowledged the best climber in Europe, Coolidge surreptitiously changed some of the "Noes" to "Ayes"! "Yes, I *cheated* Mummery into the Club!" he boasted.

It is a good story, but not likely to be true. For one thing Coolidge seldom attended Club meetings at that time and for another he had no liking for Mummery. Despite his Holy Orders, Coolidge was not renowned for forgiveness, and he never forgave Mummery over that business of the Aiguille du Géant. When Coolidge told Lunn the story it was probably no more than an old man trying to impress a young one.

Once elected to the Alpine Club it seemed as though Mummery had fulfilled his ambitions, for he spent the next four seasons very quietly, travelling mainly with his brother-in-law, Petherick. Having made their first crossing of the Schreckjoch, in 1889, they visited the Caucasus, the following year, where they seem to have been content to wander round Saunetia, though they did manage to make a new pass.

In 1891 Mummery was in the Graian Alps, a lovely though somewhat neglected area of medium-sized peaks on the borders of France and Italy, to the south of Mont Blanc. Little is known of his wanderings during this summer, but he and Ellis Carr, about whom we shall hear more later, climbed the Tour du Grand St. Pierre without guides and by a partially new route.

It is likely that he spent some time climbing with Martin Conway, who was also in the Graians. Conway was organising an expedition to the Himalaya, and he wanted Mummery to be one of the members, but though Mummery longed to visit the ultimate mountains, it soon became obvious that his ideas of climbing differed widely from those of Conway. Conway, rich, gifted, and ambitious, was a mountain romantic whose chief delight lay in exploration. He always wanted to be moving on, to see what lay beyond the next horizon. This was not Mummery's idea of mountaineering. If he visited the Himalaya it would be to climb, not explore.

During this quiet period Mummery was, as it were, pausing for second breath. These were vital years in which he reassessed his life and came to two conclusions. The first was that he must devote more time to his growing involvement in problems of economic philosophy, even at the expense of retiring from his tannery business. The second was his rejection of guided climbing in favour of guideless ascents—a momentous decision for one whose entire career and considerable reputation rested on his partnership with Alexander Burgener.

Guideless climbing was by no means a new idea when Mummery took it up. As long before as 1855 Hudson and Kennedy had made a guideless ascent of Mont Blanc, and in 1876 three English climbers—Cust, Colgrove and Cawood—startled everybody by climbing the Matterhorn without professional assistance, then regarded as a very daring thing to do. But, of course, the older climbers were against this new "rashness" and when the Rev. A. G. Girdlestone published a book called *The High Alps Without Guides* in 1870, it provided them with excellent ammunition for their salvos of criticism. Girdlestone, unfortunately, made many mistakes during his expeditions, mistakes which a good guide would have avoided.

Nevertheless, guideless climbing gained in popularity, and in the seventies the Pilkington brothers, with their cousin Frederick Gardiner, showed that skilful mountaineers could manage even difficult climbs without guides, quite safely.

One of the reasons for the rapidly gaining popularity of guideless climbing was that the new generation of mountaineers were in many respects more proficient than their elders. Especially were they good at rock-climbing, which, of course, exactly suited the needs of the times, since most of the major new expeditions were on steep rocks like those of the Géant and Grépon.

In the eighties new men came from the northern counties of Britain where they had discovered that it was not necessary to go to the Alps in order to learn about the difficulties of steep rock. The Lake District, Wales and Scotland have crags which give climbs shorter than those in the Alps, but lack nothing in fierceness. In between their annual Alpine seasons, the keenest spirits paid frequent visits to Wasdale Head or Pen y Gwryd, and at Christmas or Easter the two inns were crammed with the cream of British mountaineers.

Mummery, who lived in Dover, which is about as far away from mountains as it is possible to get, played only a small part in British climbing developments. He climbed on the chalk cliffs near his home and contributed a chapter on the subject to Haskett-Smith's *Climbing in the British Isles*, but apart from this, some scrambles in Scotland, and the second ascent of the notorious Great Gully of Wastwater Screes, he bothered little about British climbing. The Lake District was then the leading centre, and what Mummery saw of it, he did not particularly like.

"Once upon a time a celebrated climber of Alpine repute came to Wasdale for the first, alas! also for the last time," wrote his great friend, Norman Collie. "'Climbing in the Caucasus', Mummery said, 'was easy and safe; in the Alps too it was usually easy and safe, though sometimes difficult; but climbing as practised at Wasdale Head was both difficult and dangerous!'"

In the early July of 1892 Mummery, Petherick and Miss Lily Bristow journeyed to Chamonix where they found assembled some of the most adventurous spirits of the new guideless climbing movement. There was Ellis Carr with whom Mummery had climbed the previous summer, conqueror of the difficult Pic Sans Nom on the west ridge of the Verte and fresh from his daring hand traverse on the North Climb of Pillar Rock; Godfrey Solly, a constant companion of Carr's, who led the first ascent of the formidable Eagle's Nest Ridge on Great Gable, and C. H. Pasteur with his sisters—a well-known mountaineering family.

Dominating the group, however, were three men with whom Mummery was to form deep and lasting friendships, and with whom he was to share his greatest adventures.

First among these, in age and experience, was William Cecil Slingsby, a Yorkshire squire whose passion for climbing was scarcely rivalled by Mummery himself. A handsome, stocky figure with a small silken beard combed to a meticulous point, Slingsby was one of the earliest devotees of climbing on British crags and he had taken part in many of the most famous first ascents. A keen pot-holer as well, Slingsby played an important part in the formation of many British climbing and pot-holing clubs, and his tireless work in this direction has often earned him the name, Father of British Mountaineering.

Slingsby's greatest love was Norway. Of Norse ancestry himself, there was something about the wild peaks of that northern land that appealed to him irresistibly, and he returned there time and again. He was certainly the Father of Norwegian Mountaineering. His charming personality won him friends wherever he travelled, and it was often said that Norway had two patron saints—St. Olaf and Cecil Slingsby!

Second to Slingsby in this indomitable trio was the tall, lanky, John Norman Collie, a man who looked for all the world like those pictures of Sherlock Holmes which were appearing in the *Strand Magazine* at that time. Like Holmes, Collie had a prominent nose, cadaverous cheeks, and he puffed incessantly at a large curly pipe, even when climbing. By birth he was a Scot, though he had lived most of his life in the south of England, where, at this time, he was science teacher at Cheltenham Ladies' College—a job he disliked intensely. Later on he was destined to become a very famous scientist: he was the discoverer of neon gas and the first man to apply X-rays to medical purposes.

Collie frequently climbed with Slingsby and, like the latter, played a considerable part in the early days of British climbing.

Collie was ten years younger than Slingsby, more of an age with the third and final member of the team, Geoffrey Hastings. Hastings was a muscular man of great determination, renowned both for his rapid step-cutting and his ability as a campfire cook. The others tended to regard poor Hastings as the "maid of all work"—his was the heaviest sack, he did all the cooking and generally seemed to catch any rough job that was going. That he bore it all with fortitude says a lot for his quiet habits, but it must not be assumed that Hastings was any less able as a climber than the others—far from it. In his first Alpine season he had led a guideless ascent of the Dru, a remarkable achievement for a "beginner" even today, and of course, he climbed at home with Slingsby and Collie, and like them, took part in many first ascents. Indeed, it was Slingsby who first introduced Hastings to climbing and if the latter always seemed to take an inferior place it was simply because his retiring disposition made him avoid the limelight which fell on his three companions.

In the entire history of Alpine climbing, before or since 1892, there can seldom have been gathered together in one place such a galaxy of outstanding talent. Each and every one of the men assembled that year in Chamonix was a leader in his own right, a man who had made daring first ascents either at home or abroad, a man capable of tackling any climb in the world that had been done at that time. It was an assembly such as Mummery had always dreamt of: a company of brilliant equals.

Yet in any such company one man always stands out from the others, not perhaps because he is more skilful than they but because he has within him a certain fire, a driving force, an *élan*. Even amongst equals such a man becomes their natural leader, and Mummery was such a man. Despite the greater experience and wisdom of Slingsby, the imperturbable skill of Collie, the strength of Hastings, it was to Mummery that they all looked for leadership.

Mummery's first outing was with Carr, Slingsby and Solly: a reconnaissance of the north face of the Aiguille du Plan; an expedition he and Carr had discussed in England.

The Aiguille du Plan is the second highest of those rocky needles which run in a continuous wall from the Charmoz to the Midi, seeming to hang suspended over the valley of Chamonix. These are the true "aiguilles", and though their nearness to the village makes them an attractive proposition, nearly all of them require considerable skill on the mountaineer's part, because they are incredibly steep and difficult. Nevertheless, the major summits had all been attained before 1892, though in the case of the Aiguille du Plan, the stupendous north face, which looks down on the valley, was still virgin.

The face overlooks the tiny Glacier de Blaitière, and forms, with the Blaitière itself, a sort of large cwm or hollow in the ridge. This hollow is in two tiers. The lower tier is occupied by the Blaitière glacier; then, above a rock wall, there is another small patch of ice on the left and a long, very steep cascade of ice called the Glacier du Plan on the right, leading to the very summit of the Aiguille.

It was apparent to the four friends, as they looked at the face, that the first major difficulty would be in getting from the lower glacier to the upper one, over the rock barrier. They knew that some twelve years previously the great guide Emile Rey had solved this by a dangerous sortie on to the small left-hand glacier, but that having got there he found it a blind alley and had been forced to retreat. What was really needed was a way directly on to the long stretch of the Glacier du Plan.

Immediately below the Glacier du Plan there is a tongue of rock stretching down, like a great whale's back, to the Blaitière Glacier. It seemed to the reconnaissance party the logical way to reach the face, but they were under no illusions as to its difficulty. Nevertheless, the only alternative seemed far worse—a narrow, exceedingly steep ice gully on the immediate left of the whale-back. If the north face of the Plan was to be conquered at all, then one or other of these difficulties had to be faced—and the tongue of rock seemed by far the more inviting prospect.

On the left side of the rocks they saw a series of chimneys, which they reckoned might take them to the crest. At once, even before they touched a single rock, their difficulties began, for they discovered that the slopes up to these chimneys were hard ice, and not the easy snow they had hoped for. Every step had to be hewed out with their axes, and progress was extremely slow.

Consequently, the day was already well advanced by the time they reached the rocks and any hope they had of making up for lost time was quickly dispelled by the chimneys.

The climbing was difficult and consequently slow. They were aiming for a gap in the ridge, marked by a conspicuous tower on its lower side, and they hoped that once they had turned the tower and crossed the gap they would be able to follow the ridge easily to the point where it joined the main face of the Plan. But, as time slipped by, the practicability of this scheme grew less and less, and in the end it was decided simply to turn (or by-pass) the tower, in the hope that they might get a view of what lay ahead.

To speed things up, Mummery and Carr slipped off their rucksacks, and leaving their friends behind raced ahead to try to turn the tower. But even that proved beyond them. The tall pinnacle was completely inaccessible, and when they tried to by-pass it on its left they found themselves facing an almost holdless slab. Both men tried it in turn, both agreed it would "go", yet neither was prepared to commit himself, knowing full well that retreat might prove impossible. Perhaps if it had been a full-scale assault they were making, not just a reconnaissance, they might have forced it: as it was they turned back, firmly convinced that the whale's back was *not* the way to climb the Plan. Ironically enough, years later this was the very route chosen by the party of French climbers who made the present north-face route.

As Mummery's party retreated down the glacier on their way to Montenvers, racing the oncoming darkness, they cast many a dubious glance back at the Plan. Now they had ruled out the rock rib they were left with only one alternative—the fearsome looking couloir.

It was obvious that the couloir was going to be an ice climb of some magnitude; about a thousand feet at an angle varying from thirty degrees to fifty degrees, they reckoned. In preparation for this they took the precaution of sharpening their ice-axes on the hotel grindstone before setting out again the next afternoon.

The party was now reduced to three—Mummery, Slingsby and Carr—since Godfrey Solly's holiday was at an end. Their plan was to bivouac near the base of the mountain so that they could attack the couloir as early as possible, thus allowing themselves time to reach the summit, but this plan did not work out quite as they expected. Their porter, who carried the tent and other bivouac gear, made such a miserable crossing of the boulder-strewn slopes en route that they were forced to bivouac near the Nantillons Glacier, somewhat short of their objective.

Though the bivouac went well—it was a fine moonlit night— it was interesting because it was the first time that the famous

Mummery Tent was used. This was a light, easily portable ridge tent constructed of fine silk, and designed to replace the somewhat cumbersome Whymper Tent which had been the standard mountaineering tent for the past twenty-five years or so. In those days, of course, lightweight camping as we know it today was virtually non-existent, and there was not the wide range of tent patterns that a modern camper can choose from. A climber, or explorer, used the standard pattern, or designed his own, and Mummery was the first to improve on that of his predecessor Whymper. Ellis Carr was not very impressed at first: "It was necessary . . . on entering or leaving the tent to adopt that form of locomotion to which the serpent was condemned, to avoid the risk of unconsciously carrying away the whole structure on one's back," he wrote.

The tent was part of Mummery's changing ideas about climbing. Gone were the long night marches from the valley hotel—much better to bivouac high up, near the next day's climb. Even the club huts, then being built in many parts of the Alps, were too low for his fancy: "During all the years I spent climbing with Mummery only twice have I slept in a hut with him," confessed Collie.

Mummery had devoted a great deal of thought to climbing-equipment: besides his tent he introduced the use of a thinner rope and tennis shoes on difficult rock climbs; nor were wooden wedges and iron pitons unknown to him—shades of modern rock-climbers!

Perhaps his most unusual inventions, however, were Mummery Nails. These ingenious devices were sharp spikes which could be secured into a boot sole in order to provide a better grip on steep ice. In this way they helped the climber on ice, yet they were not as cumbersome as the crampons of those days, and could be left in place even when the ice gave way to rock. Carr wore them on the Plan and was very impressed by them, but they never really caught on as a fashion, and, of course, they would be useless today when boots have rubber soles and modern crampons are so very light.

The three friends left their tent at 3 a.m. on the morning of the 13th. The weather was good, the night moonlit and full of stars. Steadily they trudged their way up the now familiar Blaitière Glacier until, in the pale light of dawn, they stood at the foot of the great ice-couloir.

The couloir was in two parts, divided down its middle at

about half its height by a rib of rock. Above, they could see that it steepened to almost sheer verticality, and above that again towered banks of ugly seracs. The couloir was obviously a place for avalanches, but it was also the only way.

They crossed the bergschrund on the left, hard by the rocks on that side of the couloir, then traversed over steep ice to the central rib. This was steep and loose, but quicker than climbing the ice, so they kept to it until it came to an end, pausing only where a gap in the rocks allowed them to rest for a light breakfast. When the rocks ended they were forced into the left-hand branch of the couloir—all were agreed that the opposite branch was suicidal.

So at last they were fairly to grips with the ice they had feared, and for hour after hour, with occasional changes of leadership, they hacked their way up the unremitting slope.

The angle was a fairly uniform fifty degrees, but within a hundred feet of the top it suddenly steepened in a dramatic fashion to sixty or seventy degrees, and they halted to consider their position.

On the left, the rock wall of the couloir bulged in wet overhangs, on the right lay only dangerous slopes of the other branch of the couloir. Either way they must follow their chosen line, or retreat.

Retreat was not to be contemplated, though the wall of ice looked fearsomely steep. Mummery, however, quietly announced that he was ready to lead it, and in preparation for this 100 feet of thin rope was doubled and attached to the 80-foot rope they were already using, this giving them 130 feet of rope to run out. Neither Slingsby nor Carr questioned Mummery's ability to climb the ice-wall for a moment: "Amongst Mummery's other mountaineering qualifications," wrote Carr, "not the least remarkable is his power of inspiring confidence in those who are climbing with him."

Mummery set off and was soon reduced to cutting single-handed, hanging on to the ice with his left hand in holds he had cut specially for that purpose. He was directing his efforts towards a single projecting rock at the head of the couloir, and as he approached it the angle of the ice steepened still more until the last twelve or fourteen feet were virtually perpendicular. Never once did Mummery pause or falter: it was, said Carr, "the most extraordinary feat of mountaineering skill and nerve it had ever been my privilege to witness."

When their leader reached the jutting stone and disappeared from view his two companions confidently expected to be called to follow, but the summons did not come. Mummery just went on chipping away, climbing higher and higher, until at last even the doubled rope had to be undone and let out singly. At last, 120 feet above his companions, he halted and made a stance. The pitch had occupied two hours: it was the finest ice climb ever led by an amateur, and much more akin to modern standards than to anything that had been done previously.

They had been on the move now for several hours since their sketchy breakfast and so, prompted by pangs of hunger, they cut upwards towards their left where some jutting rocks gave sufficient platform for a rest. Then it was on again, up the unremitting ice, Mummery once more in the lead.

Another rib of rock helped them on their way for about eighty feet but then it was once more on to the ice, chopping away, forming step after endless step.

It seemed to them at this stage that the steep rock walls forming the face of the lower summit of the Aiguille du Plan, called nowadays the Dent du Crocodile, would offer the quickest means of ascent, since the Plan glacier itself was just wave after wave of tottering seracs requiring hours of hard and possibly dangerous step cutting, and time was running short.

But the rocks proved illusory. They were steep and difficult and interlaced with ice patches so that the cutting of steps had to continue. Daylight slipped into dusk and still they had not reached the main ridge of the Plan, let alone the summit.

At last darkness forced a halt. Cramped together on a tiny ledge they prepared to bivouac for the night. Their boots were wet through, so they removed them. Their stockings too were removed and wrung dry. Carr put his feet into his rucksack for warmth (a modern climbing trick), but the others seemed content to replace their wet boots and risk frostbite. So that they would not fall off their ledge during the night they hitched the rope round a rock and tied it round themselves. Thus protected they prepared to spend a miserable night, the air getting colder every hour, chilling them through to the marrow, whilst far, far below, the lights of Chamonix mocked them with the thoughts of civilised comforts.

Under such conditions sleep is virtually impossible. Remember that these men were not wearing the quilted *duvet* that cossets the modern climber with layers of warmth-preserving eiderdown, nor did they even have windproof anoraks, but just ordinary jackets such as might be worn by any country-goer of the time—"the coat I was wearing was not lined", Carr noted. So confident had they been of success that even such extra clothing as they possessed was left with the tent on the glacier far below. Had the weather turned bad they would almost certainly have perished: as it was they suffered acute discomfort. So they sat out the night, the kindly Slingsby hugging Mummery's thin frame to keep him warm.

It was three tired, cold and hungry men who prepared to continue their ascent next morning. They had nothing to drink (thirst is always a problem on a big mountain climb), precious little to eat, and the rope was frozen into intractable kinks.

Mummery took the lead and advised the others to catch some more sleep whilst he cut the steps. This they did for about half-an-hour, then followed painfully in their leader's wake.

But the climbing did not become easier as they had hoped. Steep ice-slopes were followed by short, smooth rock risers. At last Carr, who was feeling all in, cried "Halt."

As they stood perched on the steep face of the Plan they held a council of war. Carr was finished and called for retreat—but retreat meant the descent of 3,000 feet of very steep ice, including the notorious couloir. Could it be done? Mummery was for pushing on, even going so far as to unrope and solo ahead on a daring reconnaissance, only to return dejected with the news that the mountain continued to be difficult for as far as he could see.

There was nothing for it but to go down. It was a little after 5 a.m.

Slingsby went down first, with the tired Carr in the middle and Mummery last, as anchor. They had hoped to race down the steps they had cut on the way up, but to their intense dismay most of them were filled by wind-blown snow or melt water and needed recutting. This was where Slingsby proved his towering reserves of strength and endurance. Crouched forward, hour upon hour, chipping away at the ice, he could still say, "It certainly is a glorious climb."

Every step brought them nearer the terrible couloir, the memory of which filled them with dread. They thought of avoiding it by making towards the top of the whale-back, but the first formidable sight of this monster made them change

eir minds again. Better the devil you know than the one you
on't know!

At the head of the couloir they hitched a rope round a spike of
ock and let Mummery down to refashion the steps, a job he
olunteered to do. Dead tired, Slingsby and Carr held their
ader whilst he disappeared over the steep edge. He was gone
n hour. When he returned he and Slingsby lowered Carr to
fety, then Slingsby in turn descended.

Now it was Mummery's turn. He could have left the rope
ed to the rock above and swarmed down it in safety, but that
ould have meant abandoning the rope, and this he had no
ntention of doing. Instead, rejecting its aid altogether, he
oolly descended the steep ice as though he were merely step-
ing down some painter's ladder. The privations of the past
wo days seemed not to have affected him in any way.

The rest of the descent was relatively simple, though Carr
vas cut by a falling stone, as though the mountain was determined to add injury to insult. It was 5.55 p.m. when they finally
cleared the bergschrund, and 10.30 p.m. when they reached
heir anxiously waiting friends at Montenvers—just fifty-four
hours after their departure.

A year later Mummery returned to the Aiguille du Plan,
together with Slingsby, Collie and Hastings. This time he
shunned the Blaitière cwm altogether, choosing instead to
attack the mountain from the south-west, by the Pèlerins
Glacier. In this way he gained the crest of the high ridge which
divides the Pèlerins from the Blaitière and from there he was
able to traverse on to the upper slopes of the Plan Glacier and
so to reach the summit. It was the first traverse of the Aiguille
du Plan.

Though the climbing was difficult and exciting it had not the
same drama as that of the previous season. One thing though—
it enabled them to see just how near success they had been
when they turned back—scarcely three hours from the summit!

CHAPTER EIGHT

AN EASY DAY FOR A LADY

FREED FROM THE yoke of following a guide, backed by a trusted band of talented companions, Mummery was now reaching the pinnacle of his great powers. Martin Conway, who knew him well during these years, has left behind a vivid impression.

"He stands out amongst climbers as a mountain genius. There existed between him and any mountain an instinctive understanding. He knew mountains as some men know horses. He seemed born to climb them, though physically he had not the aspect of an athlete. His body was light and slender. He suffered from some weakness of the spine which disabled him from weight carrying but did not otherwise impede him. His limbs were long and the extremities extraordinarily sensitive and serviceable. He was like a spider on steep rocks to which he seemed to adhere by magic. He was tall and could outreach most men of his height. It was enough for him to have support with a toe on some almost invisible inequality and an extended finger or two at arm's length over some little crack or ledge: thus he could worm himself upwards. He had great muscular strength in arms and legs, and little weight of body for them to raise. He knew by instinct or long experience whether his points of adhesion were sufficient for momentary safety. I doubt if he ever slipped. He always had complete confidence. Nothing flurried or hurried him. He could endure any amount of cold, and would sit out a night in the open at any level. He would stay in bitter frost waiting where he happened to be till dawn enabled him to proceed. Arrived on a summit at any hour of the afternoon, he would adventure a descent by an untried route with the certainty of being benighted.

"Routes old or new were nothing to him. He took his own way and was as capable of leading as the best of guides.

"Though taking reasonable precautions, he loved danger for its own sake, and would willingly accept a margin of unavoidable risk.

"The finest climber of his or any preceding generation. . . ."

After his two-day adventure on the Aiguille du Plan in 1892,

MONT BLANC The ordinary route is along the skyline on the right, the Brenva face is on the left. Notice how the mountain completely dwarfs the Requin–Plan ridge in the foreground. (*Photo C. D. Milner*)

MUMMERY LEADING THE MUMMERY CRACK The historic photograph taken by Lily Bristow during "an easy day for a lady". (*Courtesy Alpine Journal*)

NANGA PARBAT (Photo Royal Geographical Society)

Mummery turned his attention once again to the Grépon. Eleven years had passed since he had made the first ascent with Burgener and Venetz, but such was the aura of difficulty surrounding the peak that it had been climbed only four times since.

In 1885, Henri Dunod, a noted French alpinist, had made the second ascent after repeated attempts, but he used the old approach from the south, the so-called C.P. route. His guides were Chamonix men and so, naturally, this southern route became the accepted way for anyone trying to climb the mountain, and the three other attempts up till 1892 had all been done this way, including the first guideless ascent by a party of Englishmen.

Mummery's route had never been repeated. He intended to rectify this omission, and moreover, by descending the C.P. route, to make the first complete traverse of the mountain. It was a logical plan, for if ever a mountain was designed for traversing, that mountain is the Grépon.

So on a cold, blustery day—August 18th, 1892—Mummery, accompanied by Hastings, Collie and Pasteur found themselves at the head of the Charmoz-Grépon couloir. For a short time Mummery could not remember exactly where the crack lay which proved the key to the ascent, then he found it and the party gathered together to regard the formidable fissure.

How Mummery's thoughts must have gone winging back to the day Burgener and Venetz had scaled the formidable crack and he had come up last "like baggage" as he put it. Since then nobody had climbed it: now he had to make the second ascent, but this time as leader.

The bottom of the crack bulges awkwardly, so Hastings gave him a shoulder to start, but after that he was on his own, fighting his way up the difficult fissure. About half-way, there is a resting-place; a diminutive ledge where Mummery paused for breath before tackling the next part of the crack. With scarcely anything to hold on to, he began to wedge and wriggle his way up until after what seemed an eternity, better holds appeared and, to the cheers of his companions, he pulled himself on to the easy ledge below the Kanones Loch.

The others came up one by one on the rope, struggling with the crack, and gasping their congratulations to Mummery on their arrival. It was a considerable achievement: at one blow Mummery had advanced the status of the amateur to equal the best of guides, and he had raised the standard of high Alpine rock-climbing more nearly to that of crags in Lakeland and the Dolomites.

Nothing could stop them now! They raced along to the final gap before the summit gendarme, and fixed a rope down which to slide. Each in turn went spinning down to the little col, Mummery taking the leader's place as last man.

When his turn came he slid down the rope until a small foothold allowed him a moment's rest. With regained breath he was about to continue his slide, but as he grasped the rope he was horrified to feel it slide down towards him. For an instant he wobbled and nearly fell off, but with his superb reflexes he regained his balance, much to the relief of his anxiously watching friends.

But, how was he to descend? It seemed impossible to climb down such a blank wall, and the rope, which had jammed again, was no longer to be trusted.

It was Collie who spied a line of meagre holds which offered a chance of escape. Guided from below, Mummery climbed down, holding the rope gently, ready to grasp it as a last resort if he should slip. Fortunately, such an eventuality did not take place, and in a few minutes he had rejoined his anxious companions.

Above them towered the final pinnacle, and in it was the forbidding black streak of the Venetz Crack. It was a formidable proposition—harder even than the Mummery Crack, but they were determined to climb it. Then Pasteur, who had taken part in the first guideless climb of the mountain by the C.P. route, recognised their surroundings and led them off, round the summit gendarme to a much easier crack he knew off—the one Dunod had used to get to the top.

So they completed their ascent by Dunod's route and not Venetz's. It is fascinating to speculate what would have happened if Pasteur had not intervened at the last moment— would Mummery have managed to climb the Venetz Crack?

Their descent by the C.P. route proved a comparatively simple affair. The traverse of the Grépon was complete, and from that day to this it remains one of the most popular climbs in the Alps, still proudly graded as *Difficile* after three-quarters of a century of climbing progress.

Between July 14th, when he made his attempt on the north face of the Plan, and August 18th, when he made the traverse of the Grépon, little is known of Mummery's doings. He crossed the Col de Triolet with Petherick on August 1st, according to the diary of Sir George Morse (who had made the first guideless ascent of the Grépon a few days before Mummery's traverse), but where he was going nobody knows.

One thing is certain: this month was not spent in idleness. It was probably during this period that he made his attempt on the east ridge of the Grandes Jorasses—the famous Hirondelle ridge.

The Grandes Jorasses (13,807 ft) is one of the most impressive of the Chamonix mountains, with a tremendous north face which is the setting for some of the hardest modern climbs. The peak was first climbed by Whymper as long ago as 1865, who found the only really easy way to the top, using a complicated route on the S.W. face; but subsequently attacks on the two principal ridges, east and west, were repulsed time and again.

For his attack, Mummery abandoned his guideless principles and teamed up with the great Courmayeur guide, Emile Rey. Rey was probably the only guide of the time who could claim to match the legendary Burgener himself in skill, and Mummery knew this.

Unfortunately, conditions for the climb were not good. They had to exert all their icemanship on verglassed rocks, and like other good climbers before and after them, they could not pass the crux of the ridge—a deep notch beyond which is a steep and difficult wall. Like the Furggen ridge on the Matterhorn, the Hirondelle ridge of the Grandes Jorasses was too difficult for the period—it was not climbed until 1927 or thirty-five years after Mummery and Rey tried it.

Not all of Mummery's climbs during 1892 were as desperate as the north face of the Plan or the Hirondelle ridge. Towards the end of August he led a large, gay party on a traverse of the Charmoz. Ellis Carr was there, and two ladies accompanied the party—Miss Pasteur and Miss Bristow.

Although lady alpinists were not at all uncommon by the closing years of the nineteenth century, Miss Lily Bristow was different from most. Taking her cue from Mary Mummery, she rejected the usual "ladies' peaks" like the Breithorn, and went for climbs which at that time few men, let alone women, would attempt.

She had, of course, an excellent tutor. When Mummery's wife gave up serious climbing, Lily Bristow seemed to take her

place, and from her letters home it is obvious that she and
Mummery made many climbs together, even before the
Charmoz.

The summer of 1893 saw Mummery's small world complete.
At Chamonix that year he had his wife, Lily Bristow, and the
"three musketeers"—Collie, Slingsby and Hastings. Even with
Alexander Burgener—staunch companion that he was—
Mummery had never achieved the sort of happy relationship
which he now found, for there was always that barrier between
guide and employer, no matter how slight, which did not exist
between equal friends. In a sense the old A. F. Mummery of
the Zmutt and Col du Lion days was already a legendary figure
of the past—Herr Mommerie had become, quite simply, Fred.

Already the stuffy formalities of the mid-Victorian period
were dying as a new century approached. Mummery and his
companions, like thousands of other young men and women,
welcomed the change and took advantage of it. They were
informal, gay, and witty, and though they tried to outdo one
another in looking after the welfare of the ladies, they were
quite prepared to allow Lily Bristow to share their bivouacs
whenever it proved necessary. She did not mind one bit, being
a very "modern" young lady.

In many ways Mummery's little group was much more akin
to modern climbers than they were to their immediate predecessors, both in outlook and ability. In this latter, of course,
they were unequalled in their day, as they rapidly proved.

Though Miss Bristow was never allowed to accompany the
four men on any of their major new climbs (probably much to
her annoyance, for she was a spirited young woman) they had
no qualms at all about her climbing ability, and in 1893 they
agreed that she should accompany them on a repeat of the
Grépon traverse. She, in turn, announced her intention of
making a photographic record of the climb—no mean feat with
the heavy plate cameras of those days.

On the evening of August 4th, Mummery, Hastings and
Miss Bristow bivouacked near the Nantillons glacier ready for
an attempt on the Grépon next day. They sat and watched the
stars come out then retired to their eiderdown sleeping-bags
and sheepskin rugs. Miss Bristow thought the six by four tent
somewhat crowded with three persons in it—little did she
realise then how comparatively comfortable she was!

At 5 a.m. next morning Hastings' inexhaustible rucksack

provided the means for a splendid breakfast which they were just on the point of finishing when Collie, Slingsby and a friend named Brodie arrived, having made an early start from Montenvers. Hastings was immediately prevailed upon to begin cooking all over again for the new arrivals, whilst Mummery and Miss Bristow went ahead to cut steps to the couloir.

The plan they had in mind was nothing more nor less than the utter subjugation of the once mighty Grépon. Not only was the traverse to be made from north to south by a lady (complete with camera), but whilst Mummery, Slingsby and Miss Bristow were doing this, Collie, Hastings and Brodie proposed to traverse it in the reverse direction. The two parties were to meet on the summit.

The whole expedition had something of the holiday atmosphere about it, and why not, seeing that the participants no longer held the formidable Grépon in awe? But the mountain had some nasty shocks in store for them—the weather had been continuously bad for the previous five days, and the normally easy Charmoz-Grépon couloir was loose and dangerous. The rocks, too, were coated with ice, and because the couloir is on the west side of the ridge, out of the warmth of the early morning sun, the climbers had a miserably cold ascent.

However, after some wanderings and a rest they once again came to the Mummery Crack. With Miss Bristow and her camera perched on a suitable ledge, the tripod secured, and a photographic plate in position, Mummery began again to climb his famous pitch.

The crack was ice-coated and the take-off, always one of the most difficult moves on the pitch, proved virtually impossible. Mummery's hands were cramped with cold due to the icy holds and though he made a start, he found his fingers so numb that he was glad to get down again in safety.

Seeing how matters stood, Slingsby came to the foot of the crack with him to give him a shoulder over the first awkward bit. Above, the rocks were drier and Mummery reached the resting-place—about half-way up—without much trouble, though once he started again he found hard-packed snow in the crack, which he was forced to remove by the novel, but painful, method of using his elbow as an ice-axe!

Miss Bristow, meanwhile, had been watching proceedings with the eye of a true photographer. Choosing her moment, she exposed the plate. The result of her efforts can be seen facing

page 88. It is the only known photograph of Mummery in
action.

As a matter of fact, during the course of the climb, Miss
Bristow took six photographs, one of which was a failure.
Unfortunately, all trace has been lost of the remaining plates—
they would probably have given a unique record of Mummery
traversing the Grépon.

Quite apart from her photography, Miss Bristow was enjoy-
ing herself immensely and finding the Grépon an exciting
proposition. "I have often felt on the climbs," she wrote to her
family the very next day, "that if I had sufficient knowledge
and pluck I could have done it myself, but this climb was
something totally different. It was more difficult than I could
ever imagine—a succession of problems, each one of which was
a ripping good climb in itself . . . Fred is magnificent, he has
such absolute confidence, I never once had the faintest squirm
about him even when he was in the most hideous places, where
the least slip would have been certain death. . . ."

They reached the final peak without sighting the other party
and Slingsby was somewhat concerned, but as it turned out he
need not have worried. Collie, Hastings and Brodie were
snugged up on a platform of the C.P. route, so overcome by
laziness that they had not even tried the final awkward pitch
separating them from the summit. In fact, Collie and Hastings
declined to go up even when proffered a rope from above, since
they had been up before and time was getting on. Brodie
however, was hauled up and joined the summit party, there to
congratulate the first lady to climb the Grépon.

By the time they descended to the others and had finished a
typical Hastings repast, the evening was drawing in. Mist came
up and soon it began to rain, so they hurried their way down
the Nantillons Glacier. But the darkness and the rain caused
them continually to lose their way and it was a miserable bunch
of climbers who finally reached the little tent. Mummery had
lent Miss Bristow his waterproof and she was the only dry
member of the party. It was 11 p.m. Tired and soaked, they
could go no farther and so *all six* crammed themselves into
Mummery's tent. Only Miss Bristow was permitted the luxury
of lying down in her sleeping-bag—the rest huddled together in
what little space remained, until at last dawn released them
from their agony.

Two days after this came the ascent of the Plan in which

Miss Bristow took no part, but on August 10th Mummery and his friends decided Miss Bristow should climb the Petit Dru: the mountain regarded by climbers of that day as the most difficult after the Grépon.

They camped out again, of course: Mummery, Slingsby and Miss Bristow in the tent, Collie and Hastings under the lee of a boulder. At 3 a.m. they began crossing the glacier and climbing the steep rocks of the Dru to the col. Much to her delight ("It is so much more exciting"), Mummery let Miss Bristow lead, and, though this was only the easier part of the ascent, it was nevertheless a notable occasion—almost certainly the first serious lead done by a woman in the Alps.

At 5.30 a.m. they reached the Col, where they breakfasted. Shortly after, the climbing became more difficult and they all tied on to one rope because only Mummery was capable of leading some of the pitches.

They reached the summit without further incident and though they were late on the descent, managed to arrive at Montenvers by 11.30 p.m.

The local reaction to these startling climbs is well summed up by Miss Bristow in one of her letters home: "Fred's exploits here are causing a great deal of enthusiasm. His having taken a lady up the two most difficult peaks here, without guides, in the course of one week, and having sandwiched between these expeditions a totally new ascent of a very difficult peak (the Plan) is really worthy of some applause."

Their time at Montenvers was now ended, for they had planned to spend the second half of their holiday in Switzerland, climbing in the Pennine Alps. Consequently Mummery, his wife and Miss Bristow made their way over the Col de Forclaz to the Rhône valley and on to Zinal, whilst the rest of the party tackled the High Level Route to Zermatt. They expected to meet again either at Zermatt or Breuil.

Mrs. Mummery had not been feeling too well and the stuffy heat of the Rhône valley did not improve matters. She found she could not manage the short walk from Vissoye to Zinal, being obliged to ride on a mule instead, and so Mummery put off their projected crossing of the Triftjoch to Zermatt.

To fill in the time he climbed the Zinal Rothorn with Miss Bristow. It was done almost on the spur of the moment, and throughout the day he regretted having made the decision, for the Rothorn is a long way from the village whose name it bears, and Mummery disliked long walks. In fact it was only by feminine cajolery on his companion's part that the ascent was completed.

By the route they took—the north ridge—the Rothorn is not a difficult climb compared with the Grépon or the Dru, but the Swiss were much less used to guideless climbers than the natives of Chamonix and so when Mummery and Miss Bristow returned to the hotel at 9 p.m. and announced, in reply to questions, that they had climbed the Rothorn, they were met by a polite but firm disbelief. "Non, Mademoiselle, pas possible!" they told Miss Bristow. Quite obviously, the poor little English lady had mistaken some local hillock for the great mountain!

Nine days later, with Collie and Hastings, Mummery and Miss Bristow climbed the Matterhorn by the Italian ridge from Breuil. On the way down, by the same route, they were beset by a furious storm and had to fight every inch of the way to safety.

It was the last great climb that Miss Bristow and Mummery made together. The next year she climbed with guides.

Looking back on these ascents, particularly the Grépon, Mummery recalled what the great pioneer Leslie Stephen had once said about mountains.

"It has frequently been noticed that all mountains appear doomed to pass through the three stages: An inaccessible peak —The most difficult ascent in the Alps—An easy day for a lady."

CHAPTER NINE

GUIDELESS ON BRENVA

NOT ALL MUMMERY'S climbs during 1893 were "easy days for ladies", however. Right at the start of the season he broke fresh ground by a daring ascent of the Requin.

The Dent du Requin, for rock-climbers now one of the most popular of the Chamonix aiguilles, was very little known in Mummery's day. This is hardly surprising, considering that the peak is hidden from the valley by the Aiguille du Plan, and in fact, could be considered as a mere spur of that mountain, though its bristling form is quite distinctive. Nor does it show to great advantage from the Géant Glacier, and, as was so often the case in those days with peaks of a minor nature, it had no proper name. "The peak round the corner" was how it was generally referred to, and it was Norman Collie, in a burst of romantic enthusiasm, who called it Dent du Requin—the Shark's Tooth.

Because the mountain was a considerable walk from Montenvers, Mummery's party bivouacked below it on the evening of July 24th. Collie had spent the afternoon reconnoitring the steep little glacier which led up past the slabby rocks of the face, and as they lay in their sleeping-bags, waiting for sunset, they were able to gaze at the mountain and trace possible lines of attack.

So steep did the rocky face appear that a direct ascent seemed out of the question. Instead, they planned to get on to the south-east ridge by climbing the west face, then, traversing across the face on a level with a prominent patch of snow about 500 feet below the summit, reach the east ridge and follow it to the top. At first they thought the traverse from the snow patch to the north ridge might be impossible, but shifting wisps of cloud vapour and the slanting rays of the evening sun showed them that the rocks were more broken than they appeared to be at first sight. The greatest difficulty, all were agreed, would be the summit block itself.

They were not really feeling fit enough for a major climb, since they had only just arrived from England, but the prospect of fine weather had lured them out. The expedition was therefore not taken too seriously by any of them, and when

D

accounts of it came to be written, there was frequent reference
to numerous long rests, the delights of Hastings' rucksack
(Hastings carrying all the food, as usual) and the general
disinclination of one and all to get to grips with the mountain.
"One had a railway headache," they said in a note to the
Alpine Journal, "another could not go uphill, whilst a third
could not go down, and the fourth showed the greatest desire
to add to his local geographical knowledge by making, about
every half-hour, minute observations."

They left their bivouac at 3.10 a.m., and after some tricky
route-finding through the seracs and crevasses of a very broken
glacier, reached the rocks of the south-west face three hours
later. For a while they knew that the ascent would be easy,
because the west face of the Requin is comparatively broken
and several previous attempts to climb the mountain had been
made that way. And so it proved: in a little more than two-and-
a-half hours they reached the south-east ridge.

It might be wondered why Mummery and his companions,
having elected to climb the south-west face of the Requin, did
not follow it to the summit, or failing that, having reached the
south-east ridge, did not follow *that* to the summit. But these
ways had been tried by others and found impossible, and
Mummery too, thought they were impracticable.

Instead, they descended the south-east ridge towards a
curious pinnacle bearing a resemblance to a three-cornered hat,
then, at a place previously determined, they quitted the ridge
for the east face. Almost at once they found the climbing quite
different from the comparatively easy route which had gone
before. The slabs of this portion of the face were loose and
smooth and there did not seem much chance of getting across
them to the desired snow patch. The problem was solved by
sending Mummery down on the full length of the special
200-foot line he always carried. It turned out to be much easier
than he thought it would be and before long he had not only
reached the snow patch, but reconnoitred some distance beyond
it. The way ahead, at least for the next stage, seemed easy.

It was an hour-and-a-half later before the party were
collected together again, ready to continue the assault; the
time had largely been spent fixing the long rope in position to
help them on their return. Still, the day was fine and time was
of little importance, and since none of them was feeling at his
best, the more rests they had, the better they liked it. It was

1.30 a.m. before they had completed their traverse of the east
ice and reached the ridge they hoped to ascend. They were not
far from the summit.

From the snow patch, they were surprised to find the climbing more difficult than they had imagined and several times
Hastings, the "strong man" of the party, had to give Mummery a shoulder. The ridge itself offered no respite—if anything,
the climbing looked even harder.

Facing them was a square-cut tower buttressed on their side
by a steep knife-edge of rock. Mummery tackled the edge
cheval, which was straightforward enough to a man of his skill,
but the tricky move came when the knife-edge met the face of
the block.

There was no hope of climbing the block direct, it was so
smooth, but away on the right he spied a tiny ledge, outward
sloping. It was the only way—but could he reach it?

Gradually, clinging to the knife-edge with his hands, he
leant out until his right foot touched the ledge. Then, with
equal care, he let go on the ridge with his right hand and
stretched across for a tiny crack above the ledge. Now he had
to pull himself sideways, off his saddle-like perch, on to the
sloping ledge. It was a delicate move, where one slip would
have meant disaster, and it was not made easier by his uninterrupted view of the glacier several thousand feet below.

But it was the last real difficulty. Some chimneys and a flake
crack led to the top of the Requin, which they reached at
1.10 p.m.

They stayed for over an hour on the summit before com-
mencing the tricky descent. The parts which were sheer, they
roped down,* on one occasion even using a piton to help them
(produced by Hastings from his bottomless rucksack), but they
gave this up when the rope jammed and Mummery had to
waste time climbing back up to retrieve it. The passage of the
fixed rope from the east face to the south-east ridge was
particularly fraught with danger, owing to the loose nature of
the holds, and poor Collie who came up last, had all his work
cut out dodging falling missiles which hummed and whirred
like angry birds around his ears.

Once they gained the ridge, of course, it was relatively plain
sailing to the glacier, but their lackadaisical attitude during
the ascent was beginning to reap its penalties. It was 6.25 p.m.

* By means of an *abseil* or *rappel*.

before they reached the ice, and obvious that night would over-
take them before they got back to their bivouac.

Their position was unenviable. The steep slopes which they
had climbed up in the sharp frost of pre-dawn were mushy after
a day's hot sun on them and exceedingly dangerous to descend.
A new route had to be found—but how can anyone find a new
route through a complicated glacier in the dark? Mummery,
of course, was hopeless, his eyesight was bad at the best of
times, and at night he was virtually blind. His métier was steep
slabs in bright sunlight, not complicated glaciers on a dark
night. The time had come to change leaders.

Slingsby, the veteran, took control. With a skill which left
the others perpetually amazed he led them down through the
broken ice, across crevasses, over seracs, never faltering as he
turned first one way and then another, unravelling the complexities of the glacier as though he was on some route he had
done a dozen times before instead of unknown territory at dead
of night!

At last they were brought to a halt on the edge of an ice-
cliff, peering down at a black void. Was it fifteen feet high, or
fifty? They had no means of knowing. At that very moment, a
fortuitous shaft of moonlight pierced the clouds and showed
them a more level part of the glacier fifty feet below! Slingsby
led off without more ado, and before long they had descended
the ice-wall, and were on the final steep slopes to the moraines.

Helped by their Mummery spikes they made short work of
the last slopes of ice, and tumbled wearily into their bivouac at
a quarter to midnight.

Collie and Slingsby were content to remain where they were
until morning, but for some reason best known to themselves
Mummery and Hastings decided to continue their descent
through the night to Montenvers. Hastings, with his great
strength, might be excused this youthful endurance trial, but
whatever was Mummery thinking about? It must have been a
miserable journey for him. They reached the hotel at 4 a.m.
and finding the door locked, climbed in by an open window.

For some time Mummery and his companions had been
anxious to attempt Mont Blanc by its eastern slopes, the
famous Brenva face. Seen from this aspect the oldest monarch
is quite different from the easy undulating snow-slopes which
he presents to the Chamonix valley; instead, there are savage

ridges and immense ice-walls, the like of which are unequalled in the Alps.

At that time this fearsome array of ice and rock had been breached at only one point—where a long ice arête swept down from the eastern side of the mountain to the Brenva Glacier. The "Old Brenva Route" as climbers call it today, was a really historic climb done by A. W. Moore and his friends, and led by the Anderegg brothers of Grindelwald as long ago as 1865—in fact, the very day after Whymper climbed the Matterhorn. Technically, it was far in advance of its time, and in the twenty-nine years between its first ascent and 1894 there had been only four more successful attempts—in every case, an expert amateur led by a famous guide. No guideless party had even dared to think of it, let alone climb it.

What a spur to a man of Mummery's stamp! The Brenva face—guideless! It would put paid once and for all to the myth that a good amateur was not the equal of a good guide and it would advance the status of guideless climbing. For Mummery himself, who was already something of a legendary figure amongst the younger climbers, it would kill the rumour, slyly put about by his elders and technical inferiors, that he was a mere gymnast on rock. It would establish him once and for all as *the* leading mountaineer of his times.

And so, in 1894, the tightly knit little team decided to climb the Brenva face. Unfortunately, one familiar figure was missing —Slingsby had returned to his beloved Norway after an absence of three years, though the thought of the Brenva face must have sorely tempted him.

In order to reach the Brenva Glacier from which the face rises, it is necessary to cross the main watershed of the range from France to Italy, and Mummery decided to do this by means of a new approach to the Col de Triolet, which he had reconnoitred the previous year.

His intention was to climb as directly as possible from the Argentière Glacier to this Col and at first he thought he might do this under the walls of the Aiguille de Triolet itself, but this plan proved too ambitious. Instead, he was forced farther west along the ridge towards a group of peaks known as Les Courtes, until he could force his way up a steep ice-slope to the Col des Courtes. The climbing was a good deal steeper than he imagined it would be and he was glad to reach the Col des Courtes, where his attention was taken by a most striking rock aiguille—really one of a pair—on the Courtes ridge. Years later, when it became fashionable to give names to individual aiguilles, this dramatic specimen was appropriately named the Aiguille Mummery.

From the Col des Courtes, the party had to traverse round a snow cwm to the Col de Triolet, and though this proved a relatively simple matter, the whole expedition showed quite conclusively that the best way to cross the Col de Triolet was the original one via the Couvercle.

They descended in a thunderstorm to Courmayeur and spent the next day waiting for the weather to clear. As the storm was not a bad one, they judged that very little fresh snow had fallen on the upper slopes and that a start next morning would be in order. They were in no hurry, saving their strength for whatever lay ahead, so they took most of the day in reaching the island of rocks which thrust from the Brenva Glacier and which they intended to utilise as their bivouac site. Two porters were employed to carry up the gear to the site, and to take it down again after the climbers had left for their peak.

The night was calm and cold, indicating good weather for the following day, but the three climbers had found a hard lumpy pitch for the little Mummery Tent and were not altogether comfortable. They felt cramped and they ached from contact with the sharp stones beneath them, so it was with some relief when they crawled out at 2 a.m. to a welcoming fire lit by the porters, and prospect of breakfast.

An hour-and-a-half later they roped up, and, with Mummery leading, set off to climb to the upper plateau of the glacier from where they could attack the Brenva face. It was slow going, for the way was very crevassed and difficult to negotiate, but as daylight came creeping down in a pink glow, touching first the high summit then the icy face, they could see the route they had to follow.

From the steep face of Mont Blanc a long spine-like ridge protrudes at right angles into the Brenva Glacier. This ridge forms the line of attack of Moore's Old Brenva Route. It rises from a distinct rock buttress, at first quite broad, then narrows to a real knife-edge of ice until it meets the wide front of the Brenva face. Here the slopes steepen until a line of ice-cliffs, guarding the approach to the summit snows, seems to bar all possible further progress: this is the crux—this is where a climber must force his way through or face a long, hazardous descent.

There was nothing of the lazy Requin attitude about Mummery and his companions on this day—this was serious work, and they knew it. In less than two-and-a-half hours they solved the intricacies of the ice-fall which is the final stage between the lower glacier and the ridge, and they were on the ridge itself by 8 a.m.

So far, progress had been good, but when they came to the knife arête they discovered that one side was soft, dangerous snow, the other hard ice which needed step-cutting. Quite obviously they could not traverse the snowy side for fear of avalanching both it and themselves down to the glacier below, nor were they happy at the prospect of cutting steps for three or four hundred feet. Then they remembered seeing illustrations of how the old pioneers had tackled ice ridges—by the undignified but practical method of sitting astride them and shuffling along on their backsides! Realising that time was of greater importance than the niceties of technique, Mummery unhesitatingly followed the example of the pioneers.

Reaching the end of the ice arête at 9.50 a.m., and finding a level patch of snow, they took an opportunity to rest and eat, and with the steep slopes in front of them, giving them a stern reminder of what was to come, they also emptied their rucksacks of unnecessary provisions. The view from their stance was superb.

"Nature here spread before us a scene of grandeur more stupendous than any in the Alps," wrote Hastings. "Below on our right lay the steep rolling folds of the upper Brenva snowfield, on to which avalanches of new snow, made incoherent by the sun, crashed and rumbled down the slopes between the Col de la Brenva and Mont Maudit. On our left the mountain wall stretched away to the Mount Blanc de Courmayeur and the Aiguille Blanche de Peuteret, a slope of dazzling whiteness, seamed here and there by avalanche courses. High up above where we stood, and extending for over half the distance round, threatening cliffs of ice and névé stood ready, when unchained by the ordering of Nature, to crash down the 3,000 feet of ice-slope on to the Brenva Glacier. For the present the recent fall of snow covered those cliffs of ice as a blanket, protecting them from the sun's rays, and allowed us to traverse the slopes below without the slightest risk."

Hastings took the lead, to do his share of the step-cutting. They followed the line of the ridge upwards towards the ice-cliffs until, when about a third of the way from them, they bore off to their left towards what looked like a break in the mountain's defences.

The nearer they drew to the ice-cliffs, the more formidable did they appear—sixty to seventy-five degrees of steepness, they reckoned—and what they had fondly hoped to be a chink in this armour turned out to be a mere depression hardly less difficult than the rest. It was past two o'clock when they reached it.

· Mummery took over the lead again. With Hastings and Collie sheltered from the ice-chips which flew from their leader's axe, Mummery cut hand- and footholds up the steep wall. It was strenuous work, one-handed, reminiscent of the Col du Lion and the Aiguille du Plan, and it took a lot of time.

Two hours later Mummery was still nowhere near the top of the ice-wall and a vital decision had to be made. If they continued—and there was no telling how long the ice-wall might take—they would almost certainly be benighted on the summit of Mont Blanc, with little food and no shelter; not an enviable position. If they retreated, then there was still time enough to descend to the Brenva Glacier where they could find shelter and perhaps try again next day. Reluctantly, they decided to retreat.

The food they had abandoned on the ascent was carefully collected again on the way down—even a rasher of bacon Hastings had thrown into a shallow crevasse—because they would need every scrap if they were to stay another day. Down the steep slopes, back across the ice arête—it was heartbreaking to think how long they had taken toiling up, all to no avail.

But they did not descend to the Brenva Glacier. Instead, they decided to bivouac on some rocks below the ridge and so be in a favourable position for an early start next day. Not that they really had much choice, for to retreat down the Brenva ice-fall would have been extremely dangerous until the evening frosts had hardened the séracs and snow bridges, and if they waited for that to happen, it would have been hours before they reached the site of their previous bivouac. In fact, they would need to set out again as soon as they arrived back, so it was obviously ridiculous to descend in the first place. Their only problem was that in their present elevated site they were exposed to a change in the weather, but fortunately for them the weather held good.

When present-day climbers decide on an Alpine bivouac they do so armed with every defence of modern technological progress. They have, as a minimum, a *duvet* jacket—a quilted jacket filled with eiderdown—and they may well have *duvet* trousers and socks as well to keep out the numbing cold. On top of this, as wind and waterproof outer cover, they wear a long smock of tough polyurethene, whilst underneath they are kept warm by string underwear. Rucksacks, too, are so designed that an inner lining pulls out and makes the sack into a sort of sleeping-bag. For cooking they have concentrated foods, self-heating cans of soup, and incredibly light stoves, and so it is small wonder that they can last out for several nights even in extremely unfavourable conditions.

Yet despite all these new inventions a high bivouac is still an uncomfortable experience: even in settled weather the cold is so absolutely penetrating that sleep is possible only in snatches.

Imagine, then, what it must have been like for Mummery and his companions on the rocks of the Brenva ridge. They sat beneath an overhang, on a large stone which would only allow them to rest back to back. Their breeches and stockings were wet from constant contact with ice and snow, and to protect their feet from frostbite they removed their boots and tried to shove their feet into the rucksack. Owing to the way they were forced to sit this manœuvre was not altogether successful. As extra protection against the wind they wrapped their damp legs in paper bags which had once held provisions and as a final precaution they tied themselves to the rock.

Far, far below they could see the lights of the valley, and they watched as they were extinguished one by one. This contrast between the rigour of the bivouac and the tempting sight of distant comfort is one of the mental agonies of any night out on a mountain, especially when the cold starts to eat into one's marrow.

After what seemed ages, one of the party thought he saw a pale glow in the east and shouted welcome to the dawn, but, alas, a matchlight examination of a watch showed incredibly that it was still only twenty to eleven!

To help to pass the time and beat off the cold they brewed tea in a canister, using snow for water and two candles as the source of heat.

At a quarter to four dawn broke, but clouds obscured the life-giving rays of the sun. Their boots were frozen solid, and

though they tried to thaw them by burning paper and candle
in them, it was not until six o'clock that they were able to move
their cramped limbs for their second attempt to climb the
Brenva face.

They began slowly, aching from their night out, and, like the
rope, thoroughly stiff. However, the exercise soon warmed them
and they were heartened by the fact that the snow conditions
had improved overnight. Even the knife-edged arête was easier
though they still took part of it sitting astride. At 6.50 a.m. they
reached the face itself—thus, they were three hours in advance
of their time the previous day.

From the end of the ice arête they determined to take a more
direct line than the long oblique traverse they had previously
used. They went directly up towards a rib of rock, then
following this by some interesting climbing, came up to the
formidable ice-cliff.

At first they tried a weird crevasse formed by the splitting of
the ice, but instantly grew to dislike its cold interior and
abandoned it to try elsewhere. The trouble was, nowhere
suitable really existed and in the end they were forced back to
their crevasse.

This curious fracture in the cliff was filled with tumbled
blocks, acting like white chockstones above a sort of cave in the
ice. Collie, being the lightest, was deputed to climb the
obstacle, which he managed to do at his second attempt. Much
to their immense relief they found they had conquered the ice-
wall!

Soft snow now led up to the second ice-wall, the final barrier
to the summit, but this turned out to be a minor obstacle and
at 1.30 p.m. they were above all difficulties. It was three tired
men who staggered up the last thousand feet or so of gentle
snow to the summit of Mont Blanc. It was 3.18 p.m. and the
Brenva face had been conquered!

They stayed on top for only a few minutes because of a
violent wind, then, as fast as their aching limbs would allow
they plunged down the ordinary route towards Chamonix.
At 5.45 p.m. they reached the Grands Mulets where Collie
elected to stay the night. Mummery and Hastings, however,
decided to press on for the greater comforts of Chamonix,
which they reached four hours later.

This ascent of the Brenva face proved beyond doubt Mummery's powers of leadership on a major expedition. His Alpine

education was complete. Though later in the season he led the same party up the Aiguille Verte by the Moine Ridge—an expedition they all thought was new, but which had in fact been done some years previously—it was the ascent of the Brenva face which stamped on him the final seal of greatness.

Three weeks later he made his last Alpine climb, and ironically enough it was the Zmutt arête—the very climb that had first brought him to fame, fifteen years earlier.

CHAPTER TEN

DEATH OF A TIGER

THE YEAR 1894 was a momentous one for Mummery. All the various forces which directed his life seem to have gathered themselves together in one unanimous upsurge and thrust him towards the pinnacle of ambition.

As a climber he was paramount and the Alpine Club, which had once so cruelly rejected him, was about to elect him a member of the Committee. In due course he would certainly have become President. Companions, which he so desperately lacked in the early days of his climbing career, he now had in plenty—not just opportunists attracted by his fame, but true friends like Slingsby, Collie and Hastings.

It was in 1894 also that he finally decided to give up his business interests entirely so that he could devote his life to those questions of economics with which his name was already associated.

Fortunately, too, he was persuaded in that year to write an account of his best-known climbs. Primarily intended for his friends of the Alpine Club, the book was by no means a complete autobiography: just a straightforward, though highly amusing, account of his most celebrated ascents. It was published just a week before he sailed for India, so he did not live to discover how immensely popular it proved.

My Climbs in the Alps and Caucasus, gained a position in alpine literature second only to Edward Whymper's famous *Scrambles Amongst the Alps* in popular esteem. In it, besides describing his ascents, Mummery gave his philosophy of climbing—that a sense of danger was inherent in the sport and that a good climber strove to minimise danger, but could never entirely eradicate it. He poured scorn on climbers who were content to follow guides along well-beaten tracks, urging that real climbers were those who faced the unknown armed only with their skills. To John Ruskin's famous taunt that climbers treated mountains as greased poles he asked quite bluntly, what was wrong with climbing poles?

In this way Mummery put into words the feelings not only of himself but of all the young climbers who were desperately

ying to escape from the traditions and conventions which
nded to bog down the sport. He was the first climber to state
ie ideals of climbing as we know them today—indeed, he was
iuch nearer in spirit to our generation than to the majority of
eople in his own. When Ronald Clark, the historian, wrote a
ook about famous Victorian mountaineers he deliberately
ft out Mummery simply because the man was so far ahead of
is time that he could not be regarded as Victorian at all.

A prophet is seldom recognised in his own country, however,
nd though *My Climbs in the Alps and Caucasus* was avidly read by
ritish climbers it was the stories of adventure, rather than
Iummery's philosophy, which attracted them. It was left to
ontinental climbers to follow Mummery's teachings, though
nfortunately, too many forgot that the pertinent chapter of
he book is called "The Pleasures *and Penalties* of Mountaineer-
ng", and paid dearly.

On June 20th, 1895, Mummery sailed for Bombay, with
Geoffrey Hastings and Norman Collie as his companions. At
ast he was embarking on his most cherished ambition—to
limb in the Himalaya; the greatest mountains in the world.

Seventy years ago the Himalaya were virtually unknown to
he outside world. True, the Indian surveyors under Sir George
Everest had done a good job in fixing many of the principal
ieights, and specially trained natives called *pundits* had pene-
rated deep into hostile border states spying out the lie of the
and, but the immense area to be covered meant that even with
he best will in the world, the survey could not fill in details
with accuracy. Very few Europeans had penetrated the
inhospitable wildernesses of snow and ice which formed the
range, or even visited the valleys where the villages existed.
Political difficulties added to the natural ones already in
existence: states such as Tibet and Nepal were closed to Europeans entirely, whilst in the western part of the ranges, where
the Moslem religion held sway, fierce tribes, led by ruthless and
despotic chieftains, kept the whole region in more or less
continuous ferment.

Such Europeans as did penetrate into these inhospitable
regions did so in order to explore, not to climb, and although
the summit of Shilla (23,050 ft) had been reached as long before
as 1860, and Younghusband had crossed the Muztagh Pass in
1887, such high-altitude excursions were incidentals to the
main work of surveying unknown territory. Before Mummery,

there had been only two *climbing* expeditions to the Himalaya—
that of W. W. Graham who visited Sikkim and the Nanda Devi
area in 1883 (the same Graham who climbed the Aiguille du
Géant, incidentally) and the massive expedition of Martin
Conway to the Karakoram in 1892, from which Mummery had
withdrawn. Both these parties had met with modest success.

When Mummery, Collie and Hastings came to plan their
own expedition they had two limiting factors to bear in mind.
The first of these was cost, for though none of them was poor,
they were not very rich, and they would have to bear the entire
cost of the trip between themselves. This meant that whatever
peak they chose had to be fairly accessible. Secondly, their
objective was to climb a big mountain—a really big one—or
there was no point in making the journey at all: remember that
Mummery was not in the least interested in exploration for its
own sake and neither was Collie or Hastings; climbing was what
they wanted, and they looked to the Himalaya to provide a big
new peak.

One mountain filled both of these conditions. Nanga Parbat.

Nanga Parbat (26,620 ft) is the tenth highest mountain in
the world. It lies in the Punjab Himalaya, at the extreme
western end of the range, and helps to separate the beautiful
state of Kashmir from the wild northern territories embracing
the Karakoram. Around its foot bends the great Indus river,
turning at this point from a westerly to a southerly course, and
the deep valley carved by the river, together with the tremendous height of the mountain, makes Nanga Parbat one of
the most impressive peaks in all the Himalaya (picture facing
p. 89).

From Gulmarg, the hill station of Pir Panjal, one can look
across the Vale of Kashmir and see Nanga Parbat like a dream
cloud, floating high in the heavens. From across the Indus
valley it presents a much fiercer aspect —23,000 ft of ice-draped
precipice: the most dramatic mountain wall in the world.

This was the mountain which Mummery and his friends
fondly hoped to conquer. Armed as we are today with our
superior knowledge of Himalayan mountains and the effects of
high altitude we can smile at the naïve innocence of these
Victorian pioneers: they really did think that Nanga Parbat
was simply Mont Blanc on a bigger scale and that reaching the
summit was just a question of finding a convenient way up. In
a letter to his wife, Mummery wrote: "I don't think there will

be any serious mountaineering difficulties on Nanga, and the
peak is much freer from hanging glaciers than I had expected.
I fancy the ascent will be mainly a question of endurance."

The seventy years which have passed since Mummery wrote
those words have proved how wrong he was. No fewer than
seven German expeditions tried to climb the mountain
between 1932 and 1953, when finally Hermann Buhl reached the
summit alone after an incredible feat of endurance. No other
man has ever conquered Nanga Parbat, but eleven Germans
and fifteen porters lie buried beneath its snow; silent testimony
that of all the great Himalayan peaks, this is the toughest.

What a cruel irony of fate that the most approachable of
Himalayan giants should also be the most difficult! Misled, no
doubt, by the reports of the comparatively simple ascents made
by Graham and Conway, Mummery and his friends errone-
ously assumed that *all* Himalayan mountains were easy meat.
Like the proverbial lambs led to the slaughter, they were
walking right into a trap.

On July 16th they set up their provisional Base Camp at the
hamlet of Tarshing in the Rupal valley, which flanks the southern side of Nanga Parbat. It was a magnificent camp site on a
flat stretch of meadow by the Rupal torrent, overhung by
shady willows, and live with the calls of larks and cuckoos. It
might have been a scene in rural England but for the fact that
every moment of the day was dominated by the immense bulk
of the mountain they had come to climb.

After their long journey out from England, with its attendant
enforced idleness, the three friends decided that their first task
was to regain some semblance of fitness. All round were
numerous peaks, which, though nowhere near the height of
Nanga Parbat itself, were still considerable mountains, and it
was one of these that they made their first objective as a
"training climb". They failed, and much disconcerted, shifted
their attack to a lower peak. They failed again. At last, in
frustration, they climbed an insignificant rocky eminence.

Back at Base Camp they realised that the climbing in the
Himalaya was more arduous than they had at first imagined,
though they put down their failures to their being out of
condition, and the rarity of the air at high altitudes affecting
their breathing. The sad truth is that they learnt nothing from
these preliminary excursions, in particular they failed to adjust
themselves to the scale of things which was so much greater

than the Alps. Only slowly did this realisation penetrate their Alpine thinking, and then it was too late.

One thing was certain. They were never going to climb Nanga Parbat from the Rupal valley because the mountain is absolutely impregnable on that side, and they quickly realised

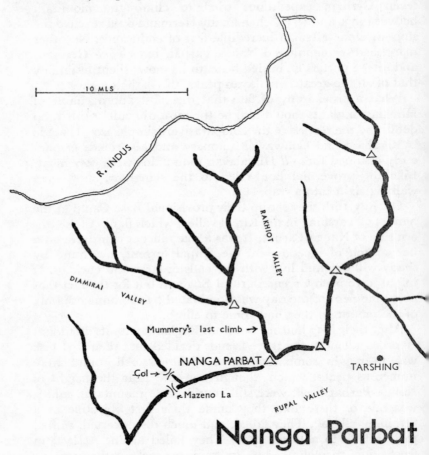

the fact. They decided that a reconnaissance of the northern side was called for, and they made this their first serious objective.

There was no difficulty in finding a way from the Rupal valley in the south to the Diamirai valley in the north, for the two were connected by a well-known pass called the Mazeno La (see map above), 18,000 feet high, which had been used for

enturies by traders and marauding tribesmen. Though not
difficult in the climbing sense it was a long, painful trudge over
an abominable rock-strewn track. Mummery and his companions hated every minute of it, and they were glad when at
long last the purgatory was over and they reached the Diamirai
river.

Their reconnaissance of the Diamirai face of Nanga Parbat
raised their hopes. "We discovered an absolutely safe way up
Nanga," Mummery wrote to his wife. "Easy glacier, up which
coolies can carry our camp, and thence onward, a broad snow
and rock ridge right up to the top. . . . I feel fairly confident of
getting up, and you need feel no anxiety of any sort."

When their reconnaissance was over, they were faced with
the prospect of returning to Base Camp over the dreaded
Mazeno La. As this did not appeal to them one little bit they
looked around to see whether the high mountain walls encir-
cling the Diamirai valley offered an alternative way home.

Luck seemed with them. On the south side of the Diamirai
valley the mountain crest dipped into a magnificent col, which
the friends at once christened the Diamirai Pass. By their
reckoning it would lead directly to the Rupal valley, cutting
out the Mazeno La.

Setting out before midnight with the aid of their glacier
lanterns they climbed up steep, broken ground until, by the
early dawn light, they spied a rock rib leading directly to the
col. Much to their satisfaction this proved an interesting climb,
and they ascended rapidly, although the col itself never seemed
to get any nearer. "These Himalaya are constructed on a scale
entirely different from the Alps or any of the ordinary snow
mountains," Collie commented, breathlessly. He was learning
fast.

At eleven o'clock a mist came down to obscure their view,
but shortly afterwards they reached what they thought was the
col and began to descend the other side. Imagine their chagrin,
however, when they discovered that they were going *back* into
the Diamirai valley! Painfully, they returned to the rock rib.

It was two o'clock when they eventually reached the col and
gazed over the other side. To their horror they saw not the
Rupal valley as they so confidently expected, but the northern
end of the Mazeno La! They had travelled three miles and
ascended to 18,000 feet in fourteen hours—all to no avail.

There was nothing for it but to descend to the foot of the

Mazeno La, then cross that pass to the Rupal valley. The very idea of this so depressed Mummery that he wildly suggested striking up from the col across a 21,000-foot peak in the hope that it would at least bring them to the summit of the Mazeno La, but Collie and Hastings would have none of it. Such a madcap idea meant benightment at high altitude, leading at least to frostbite and possibly death. In the end, Mummery agreed that the only proper thing to do was descend.

By the time they reached the foot of the Mazeno La they were very tired and hungry. There was nothing to eat save a few scraps of chocolate reserved for such emergencies. Realising that the sooner they crossed the hated pass the better, they decided to press on through the night.

As they ascended the agonising, boulder strewn track in the gathering gloom, stumbling over loose boulders, barking their shins, leg weary and famished, Norman Collie began to show his true stature as a mountaineer. Tired though he was, his gaunt lanky figure, haggard with endurance, summoned enough energy to encourage the other two.

Hastings' massive frame responded magnificently. He climbed step by step with Collie, but whereas the latter seemed able to keep going for ever at the same steady pace, Hastings visibly flagged as the night wore on.

Mummery, alas, was reduced to a pitiable spectacle. Never a good walker, the darkness of the night made his bad vision intolerable. Half blind, he would stagger a few yards at a time, then collapse prostrated amongst the boulders. For a few feet he would crawl on hands and knees, then by supreme will-power hoist himself on to his feet again to try to make the next few miserable yards before he collapsed once more. Time after time this was repeated—nobody would have believed that the poor wretch crawling on all fours was supposed to be the greatest mountaineer in the world!

They reached the summit of the pass at 8 p.m. and after a short rest, pressed on, Collie still going like a steam-engine. Hour after hour they continued down the tortuous path to the Rupal valley, until at last Collie reached the foot of the pass where a native porter was waiting with food and drink. As he fell on the food like a ravenous lion, Hastings joined him. The porter was promptly despatched up the track to succour the struggling Mummery, still some miles behind.

The time was 7 a.m. It had taken them eleven hours to

descend from the summit of the Mazeno La and they had been on the move almost without respite for *thirty-one hours*, over the roughest country in the world. Even in a region where feats of endurance were to become a commonplace, Collie's crossing of the Mazeno La remains to this day an extraordinary performance.

Not that the incredible Scot had finished—Hastings was done for, and so was Mummery, but the food and drink seemed to revitalise the lean frame of Collie. After a three-hour rest he set off alone for Base Camp, a further *seven hours*' walk, there to be greeted by Charlie Bruce with welcoming smiles and much needed bottles of Bass.

The Hon. Charles Granville Bruce was a Lieutenant with the 5th Gurkha Rifles stationed at Abbotabad, and a man destined to make a great name for himself as both soldier and mountaineer. Despite his aristocratic connections, Charlie Bruce was no *pukka sahib* who looked down his nose at the natives under his command, but a real down-to-earth character respected by officers and men alike. Nobody, before or since, understood the Gurkha soldier as Bruce did, for not only did he speak their language fluently (including the dialects), but he seemed to have had a natural affinity to the Oriental mind, so that he knew exactly how they would react in any situation. He thought the world of his tough little Gurkhas, and they, in turn, loved him like a father.

Bruce was a big man with a great zest for life. Tough as weathered oak, he had a tremendous sense of humour and his roar of laughter echoed down many a remote Himalayan valley. He would wrestle, ride, shoot, or run with any man alive, and when confined to barracks it was said that he frequently ran up some neighbouring hill just to keep in trim— *carrying his batman!*

It was also said, by the knowledgeable ones, that but for young Charlie Bruce, Conway's expedition to the Karakoram would have been a failure, and whatever the truth of this there was no denying that the young officer had an extraordinary knowledge of the Himalaya. Whereas other officers spent their leaves in the comfort of Delhi or Simla, Bruce spent his wandering in the remote quarters of the great mountains.

On these excursions he usually took two or three of his Gurkha N.C.O.'s, for Bruce realised that the Gurkha (and his peaceful cousin, the Sherpa) was a born mountaineer. In 1895, when he joined Mummery's party, Bruce brought along Raghobir Thapa and Goman Singh, two of his best men.

Mummery, in a letter to his wife, dismissed the crossing of the Mazeno La in a few words, saying nothing at all about their exhausted condition. In fact, he says that "we were from 15,000 to 18,000 feet up all day long, and felt as fresh as daisies . . .", but this was simply not true and it is probable that he was seeking to reassure Mrs. Mummery that the expedition was perfectly straightforward and safe. This is borne out by the constant references to the easy nature of the climbing, and the way which, in letter after letter, he tries to assuage her obvious fears. "I am as fit as I have ever been in my life; you need not feel the least anxiety", he writes on July 26th, and a few days later, "I hope you have not been nervous. We have run no risk of any sort. . . ."

On the 27th and 28th they made a weak attempt on Chongra Peak (22, 360 ft) but "laziness was in the air", as Collie put it, and they returned to Base.

At the end of July the Base Camp at Tarshing was struck, packed on to the coolies' backs and sent over the Mazeno La to the Diamirai valley.

The climbers, for their part, had had quite enough of the dreadful pass to last a lifetime and they were determined to force another route across the ridge separating the two valleys. They fully appreciated that they could not make the crossing in a single day, that a high bivouac would be necessary, but this time they were prepared for it. Or rather, they attuned their minds to the risk, since there was little they could do in a practical way except carry extra food.

Their ascent from the Rupal valley began by climbing steep broken moraine, continuing by a glacier which led them to a couloir. This they followed towards the crest of the ridge which they reached at 5 p.m. Bruce was not feeling at all well (he had a serious bout of mumps, though he did not know it), but Collie gave him some citrate of caffeine to alleviate the pain.

At the point they reached, the ridge was 20,150 feet high and led upwards towards a peak which was some 1,300 feet higher still. Collie judged that they could not cross the peak before darkness fell, so he proposed retreating a little way and finding a good place to bivouac for the night. Mummery, however, had other ideas. Remembering how he, Slingsby and Carr had climbed by moonlight on the Aiguille du Plan, he decided to keep going through the night, relying on a full moon to light their way. Hastings thought the idea a sound one, but the others preferred their own scheme, and so in the end Collie, Bruce and Raghobir descended, whilst Mummery and Hastings pressed on.

Unfortunately, the moonlight did not materialialise. Banks of mist swirled up from the valley, obliterating everything, so Mummery and Hastings were forced to retreat and they ended up by bivouacking just a little way above the chockstone where Collie and his companions were perched for the night. The height was 19,000 feet.

What a miserable cold night they must have spent as the sombre mists swirled about Nanga Parbat! They were without protective clothing such as Himalayan climbers of today wear —all they had were wool pullovers and tweed suits, gloves and balaclavas. The cold struck through such inadequate layers in no time, like freezing bands of steel, crushing them with its intensity. Every breath was like drawing in air from a refrigerator. Icicles grew in their beards and on their eyelashes and the numbing awful cold reduced them to complete immobility as that they sat the night through like statues frozen to their pedestals.

When at last dawn paled the eastern horizon, and the warmth of the sun's rays loosened their aching, taut muscles, they resembled old men, feeble and racked by some terrible experience. To go on was unthinkable—it was all they could do to return to the Rupal valley where everyone but Collie and Raghobir fell into a sound sleep.

As the day was still young, Collie decided that he and the Gurkha would cross the Mazeno La in search of their new camp. Almost immediately, however, it became obvious that Raghobir was in a bad way. He stumbled and fell repeatedly, and though by sheer will-power he managed to keep going he was like a man in a trance, almost unconscious on his feet. Finally he collapsed altogether and there was nothing Collie could do but wait until the others arrived some two hours later, when, between them, they carried the helpless Gurkha over the pass. It turned out that for some reason Raghobir had not eaten for two days!

Bruce left them in the Diamirai valley. His leave was almost at an end and he was still suffering from mumps. Hastings had managed to twist an ankle on the journey from Rupal, so there

were only four effective climbers left—Mummery, Collie, and
the two Gurkhas whom Bruce had left behind.

In order to reconnoitre Nanga Parbat more effectively they
determined to divide forces. Collie and Goman Singh examined
the subsidiary Diama Glacier, Mummery and Raghobir took a
close look at an intriguing system of rock ribs which form such
an obvious feature of the mountain's western face.

Setting out at midnight, Mummery and his companion
attacked the first rib and discovered the climbing was magnificent—"similar in standard to the Chamonix aiguilles". A
second rib followed the first and this too they vanquished
reaching a height of 17,000—18,000 feet. Here they decided
to turn back, though not before Mummery noted that a tent
might be established on top of the rib, and that the way ahead
offered promise of success.

Unfortunately, before anything could be done the weather
broke, confining the climbers to camp. It was decided, however,
that every effort should be made to attack the Diamirai face
by the route Mummery had discovered. During the next few
days, when the weather permitted, they managed to establish
a food dump on the second rib at 17,150 feet. Collie was amazed
at the difficulty of the climbing, which he reckoned was equal
to their climb on the west face of the Plan. Then the weather
broke again and all plans were shelved for the time being.
Mummery had high hopes of success: "I think we are bound to
have the summit," he wrote home, "as it is merely a matter of
steady training to get our wind into order."

When the weather cleared they decided that before attacking
Nanga Parbat they should climb the adjacent Diamirai Peak
(19,000 ft) for practice. Hastings had gone down the valley
for provisions and the climbing party consisted of Mummery,
Collie, Raghobir and a local porter named Lor Khan who
insisted on accompanying them. Mummery led the whole way,
and though they had an axious moment when Lor Khan slipped
on a steep ice-slope (he had no boots—only rags on his feet) they
managed to reach the summit and, by descending a different
way, they even traversed the peak. The climbing was by no
means easy, and very exposed, "just the kind of place Mummery enjoyed", Collie drily commented later, but their success
gave them fresh hopes for Nanga Parbat itself.

At 2 a.m., August 15th, Mummery, Collie, Raghobir, Lor
Khan and a hunchbacked coolie they nicknamed Richard III,

started for the upper glacier to establish what would nowadays be called Camp I. At the camp, however, Collie became ill, his iron constitution finally giving way to the poor food they had been eating of late. He returned to Base Camp with Richard III whilst Mummery led the remaining two up the first and second ribs where they spent a miserable night out. The weather became foul. It snowed quite heavily.

Next day, in thick mist, Mummery, Raghobir and Lor Khan pushed on up the third rib for about a thousand feet, where they deposited a rucksack of provisions which they fondly hoped would provide the springboard for the final assault. The height was about 20,000 feet—about 6,000 feet below the summit, which, as we now know, is much too low for a summit assault. Nevertheless, under the conditions, Mummery had done a magnificent job and it was with some relief that Collie welcomed him back to Base Camp late that night.

On the 18th they set off again, anxious to bag their peak before the weather broke for good. They slept that night at Camp I. When dawn broke, Collie was once again taken ill and he had the misfortune to remain behind, watching Mummery and Raghobir disappear up the steep rocks until they were swallowed by the drifting banks of mist.

Once again the two men spent the night on top of the second rib. It was bitterly cold, but they survived the ordeal and next day began to climb the third rib. At last they reached the deposited rucksack, then carried on. For a few more hundred feet all went well, then suddenly Raghobir stopped. He was on the point of collapse and could go no farther. There was only one thing they could do—go down.

They were well over 20,000 feet and Mummery was convinced that the way was clear to the top. What anguish there must have been in his heart when his partner collapsed! Months of effort seemed to be wasted; the cup of success dashed from his lips at the very instance of drinking.

Sadly they returned to Base Camp.

Time was running short. Holidays were almost at an end, and the weather was breaking. Already they had abandoned their first base in the Rupal valley, appalled by the unscalable precipices which Nanga Parbat shows on that side, and they had been frustrated in all their efforts on the Diamirai face too. Mummery and Raghobir had climbed splendidly—certainly some of the most difficult rock-climbing ever attempted on a

big Himalayan mountain—but it was *too* difficult for success.
What they really required was an easy snow route to the summit.

They had one hope left, and on it they made their last
gamble. One face of the mountain remained unexplored—that
of the north-west, known as the Rakhiot face, and this they
determined to examine in the hope that it might provide their
key to success.

The Rakhiot valley is separated from the Diamirai valley by
a high lateral ridge (see map, p. 112). Collie proposed that they
should descend the Diamirai valley, turn the end of the ridge
and go up to Rakhiot to a suitable camp site. It was a sensible,
prudent plan, but such a long trek was not to Mummery's
liking. Instead, he proposed to cut across the ridge directly
from Diamirai to Rakhiot.

Collie did not like the idea at all: his sound mountaineering
sense urged him against it. The ridge was steep, unknown and
subject to avalanches, and though there was a col which
Mummery optimistically called the Diamai Pass, there was no
knowing whether descent would be possible on the other side.
He advised Mummery to be very careful. Mummery laughed
at his fears. "Don't worry—I'm not going to risk anything for
the sake of an ordinary pass," he assured him.

That evening Mummery wrote to his wife. "Well, I shall soon
be on my way home. . . . Tomorrow I cross a high pass with the
Gurkhas to the Rakhiot nullah. Hastings and Collie go round
with the coolies and stores."

On the morning of August 24th, 1895, Mummery, Raghobir
and Goman Singh set out to cross the Diamai Pass. Collie and
Hastings had already departed for Rakhiot, and only Lor
Khan and Richard III remained behind to watch as the three
men, loping forward like tigers in the snow, disappeared
towards their distant goal.

The coolies turned and went down the valley. Mummery and
his companions were never seen again.

APPENDIX

MUMMERY: PRINCIPAL DATES AND CLIMBS

THOUGH IT IS very unlikely that anything further will be discovered about Mummery's climbing, there is always an outside chance that something might turn up from an unexpected source to help fill some of the mysterious blank periods of the man's life. Mr. T. S. Blakeney, whose article *Some Notes on A. F. Mummery* (*A.J.*, Vol 60) should be consulted by anyone interested in details of Mummery's life, suggests that the old registers at Swiss mountain hotels might be a possible source. The mystery is deepened by the disappearance of Mummery's notes from the library of the Alpine Club—have they been accidentally destroyed or are they still tucked away on somebody's bookshelf, forgotten?

The following list is based on Mumm's *Alpine Club Register* and shows the principal events in Mummery's life and all his known climbs.

1855
Sept. 10th   Born in Dover, Kent

1871
Sept.   Crossed the Théodule Pass

1873 or 74   Alphubeljoch, Monte Rosa (F. Anthamatten)

1874   Matterhorn

1875   Triftjoch, Matterhorn (F. Anthamatten)

1876   Mont Blanc by Mont Blanc glacier

1879
Aug. 26th   Crossed Tiefenmattenjoch from Breuil to Zermatt
Aug. 27th   Crossed Mischabeljoch from Zermatt to Saas (Burgener)
Aug. 28th   Lagginjoch (Burgener, Gentinetta)
Aug. 29th   Fletschhorn traversed by new route (Burgener, Gentinetta)

Aug. 30th	Sonnighorn traversed. 1st ascent (Burgener, Gentinetta)
Aug. 31st	Crossed Ried Pass from Saas to Zermatt (Burgener, Gentinetta)
Sept. 3rd	Matterhorn by Zmutt arête. 1st ascent (Burgener, Gentinetta, Petrus)
Sept. 6th	Dürrenhorn. 1st ascent (Penhall, Burgener, Imseng)

1880

April 6th	Rejected by A.C. ballot
June —	Col Tournanche
July 6th	Col du Lion traversed. 1st ascent (Burgener)
July 7th	Reached Courmayeur
July 12th	Crossed Col du Géant from Courmayeur (Burgener, Venetz)
July 13th–14th	Visited Grands Mulets (Burgener? Venetz?)
July 15th	Grands Charmoz. 1st ascent (Burgener, Venetz)
July 16th	Arrived at Stalden.
July 17th–18th	Attempt on Furggen Ridge abandoned. (Burgener, Venetz)
July 19th	Matterhorn by Furggen Ridge and E. face. 1st ascent (Burgener, Venetz)
July 20th	Arrived at Chamonix
July —	Attempts on Aiguille du Géant (at least two attempts) (Burgener, Venetz?)

1881

July 28th	Col du Géant (Burgener? Venetz?)
July 30th	Aiguille Verte by Couloir en Y. 1st ascent (Burgener)
Aug. 1st	Attempt on Grépon from Mer de Glace (Burgener, Venetz)
Aug. 3rd	North summit of Grépon. 1st ascent (Burgener, Venetz)
Aug. 5th	South summit of Grépon. 1st ascent (Burgener, Venetz)

1882

1883

March 7th	Married Mary Petherick

1884

1885

1886

Aug. 16th   Crossed the Bietch Pass from Bel Alp to Lötch-
ental (Mrs. Mummery)

1887
June 18th–
    July 19th   Jungfrau, Drieckhorn, Rothorn, Matterhorn
(Mrs. Mummery, Burgener, Andermatten)
July 16th   Täschhorn by Teufelsgrat. 1st ascent (Mrs.
Mummery, Burgener, Andermatten)
1888   Caucasus (names of porters omitted)
Aug. 7th   Arrived at Bezingi
Aug. 8th   Arrived at Misses Kosh
Aug. 9th   Reconnoitred Dych Tau (Zurfluh)
Aug. 10th   Ascended S.W. buttress of Dych Tau, alone
Aug. 12th   Crossed Dych Su pass. 1st ascent (Zurfluh)
Aug. 13th   Attempt on Shkara (Zurfluh)
Aug. 14th   Returned over Dych Su pass (Zurfluh)
Aug. 17th   Crossed the Zanner pass from Kosh to Miyal
(Zurfluh)
    Aug. 19th   Crossed Tuiber and Leksur passes to Chegem
valley (Zurfluh)
Aug. 20th   Arrived at Chegem
Aug. 21st   Arrived at Bezingi
Aug. 24th   Dych Tau. 1st ascent (Zurfluh)
Dec. —   Elected A.C.

1889
n.d.   *The Physiology of Industry* by A. F. Mummery
and J. A. Hobson
Aug. 17th   Crossed the Schreckjoch. 1st ascent (Petherick)
1890   Caucasus
Aug. 17th   Crossed the Fytnargyn pass. 1st ascent
(Petherick)

1891

Aug. 12th   Tour du Grand St. Pierre. (Carr)
Aug. —   Climbs with Conway

1892

July 11th	Reconnoitred north face of Aig. du Plan (Carr, Slingsby, Solly)
July 13th–14th	Attempt on north face of Aig. du Plan (Carr, Slingsby)
July 23rd	Aiguille des Charmoz traversed (Carr, Collie, Petherick, Pasteur, Miss Pasteur, Miss Bristow)
Aug. 1st	Crossed the Col de Triolet (Petherick)
Aug. 18th	Aig. de Grépon traversed. 1st traverse (Hastings, Collie, Pasteur)
Aug. —	Attempted Hirondelle Ridge of Grandes Jorasses (Rey)

1893

Easter?	Great Gully, Wastwater. 2nd ascent
July 25th	Dent du Requin. 1st ascent (Slingsby, Hastings, Collie)
July —	Col de Triolet
Aug. 5th	Aig. de Grépon traversed (Slingsby, Miss Bristow)
Aug. 7th	Aig. du Plan by W. face. 1st ascent (Slingsby, Hastings, Collie)
Aug. —	Petit Dru (Miss Bristow, Hastings, Slingsby, Collie)
Aug. 15th	Zinal Rothorn (Miss Bristow)
Aug. 24th	Matterhorn by Italian ridge (Miss Bristow, Collie, Hastings)

1894

Aug. 2nd	Col des Courtes. 1st ascent (Collie, Hastings)
Aug. 4th	Attempt on Brenva face (Collie, Hastings)
Aug. 5th	Mont Blanc by Brenva face. 1st guideless ascent (Collie, Hastings)
Aug. 11th	Aig. Verte by Moine ridge (Collie, Hastings)
Aug. 27th	Matterhorn by Zmutt arête (Abruzzi, Collie, Pollinger)

1895

n.d.	*My Climbs in the Alps and Caucasus* by A. F. Mummery

HIMALAYA

June 20th	Left England
July 5th	Arrived Bombay
July 9th	Arrived Kashmir
July 14th	Crossed Tragbal and Kamri Passes
July 16th	Camped at Tarshing Glacier
July 20th	Crossed the Mazeno La to Diamirai (Hastings, Collie)
July 22nd	Arrived Diamirai
July 23rd–24th	Crossed the Diamirai Pass and Mazeno La (Hastings, Collie)
July 28th	Explored Tarshing Glacier (Collie, Bruce)
July 31st	Attempt on a new pass to Diamirai (Collie, Hastings, Bruce, Raghobir)
Aug. 1st	Crossed the Mazeno La (Collie, Hastings, Bruce, Raghobir)
Aug. 2nd	Crossed Butesharon Pass to Diamirai. 1st ascent (Collie, Hastings, Bruce, Raghobir)
Aug. 6th	Reconnoitred Diamirai face of Nanga Parbat (Raghobir)
Aug. 11th	Diamirai Peak. 1st ascent (Collie, Raghobir, Lor Khan)
Aug. 15th–16th	Took supplies on to Diamirai face (Collie, Raghobir, Lor Kahn)
Aug. 19th–20th	Attempt on Diamirai face (Raghobir)
Aug. 24th	Disappeared on Nanga Parbat (Raghobir, Goman Singh)

BIBLIOGRAPHY

The keystone to any study of A. F. Mummery is, of course, his own immortal *My Climbs in the Alps and Caucasus*. It is, however, by no means a complete account of his climbing and it throws no light on his private life at all.

The following volumes have been consulted in the preparation of this book. The *Alpine Journal*, as always, was invaluable, but I have listed here only those articles of special importance; shorter notices, obituaries and the like I have omitted.

T. S. Blakeney, *Some Notes on A. F. Mummery* (*A.J.*, vol. 60)

Miss L. Bristow, *Letters to Her Family* (*A.J.*, vol. 53)

C. G. Bruce, *Twenty Years in the Himalaya*

E. Carr, *Two Days on an Ice Slope* (*A.J.*, vol. 16)

R. W. Clark, *The Early Alpine Guides*

R. W. Clark and E. C. Pyatt, *Mountaineering in Britain*

J. N. Collie, *Climbing on the Himalaya*

— *Ascent of the Dent du Requin* (*A.J.*, vol. 17)

Sir W. M. Conway, *Mountain Memories*

W. A. B. Coolidge, *The Alps in Nature and History*

C. T. Dent, *Above the Snowline*

C. E. Engel, *A History of Mountaineering in the Alps*

G. Hastings, *Over Mont Blanc by the Brenva Route* (*A.J.*, vol. 17)

M. Kurz, *Guide des Alpes Valaisannes*

Sir A. Lunn, *Mountain Jubilee*

— *Zermatt and the Valais*

K. Mason, *Abode of Snow*

Monte Rosa Section, *Monte Rosa 1865–1965*

A. L. Mumm, *The Alpine Club Register*

W. Penhall, *The Matterhorn from the Zmutt Glacier* (*A.J.*, vol. 9)

Guide Vallot, *La Chaîne du Mont Blanc*

G. W. Young, *Mountain Prophets* (*A.J.*, vol. 54)

Alexander Burgener's Führerbuch